STAYING ON
TOP

STAYING ON TOP

TOP

The Business Case for a National Industrial Strategy

KEVIN P. PHILLIPS

RANDOM HOUSE NEW YORK

*Grateful acknowledgment is made to the following for
permission to reprint previously published material:*

Dallas *Morning News*: Excerpt from June 17, 1983,
article by Richard Fisher. Reprinted with permission of
the Dallas *Morning News.*

Los Angeles *Times*: Adaptation of material from May 22, 1983,
Los Angeles *Times* Poll. Copyright © 1983 Los Angeles Times.
Reprinted by permission.

Newsweek: Adaptation of material from
Gallup/*Newsweek* Poll, May 1983. Copyright © 1983 by Newsweek, Inc.
All rights reserved. Reprinted by permission.

Penn-Schoen Associates: Adaptation of material from February 1983
Garth Analysis Survey. Used with permission.

U.S. News & World Report: Material from chart appearing
on September 12, 1983. Copyright © 1983 by U.S. News & World Report, Inc.
Used with permission.

Library of Congress Cataloging in Publication Data

Phillips, Kevin P.
Staying on top.

1. Industry and state—United States. 2. Industrial
promotion—United States. I. Title.
HD3616.U47P48 1984   338.973   83-43206
ISBN 0-394-53744-0

TO MARTHA

Preface

This book is essentially about America's role in the world economy and the politics of blueprinting new policies to safeguard our primacy and prosperity—to keep Dayton, Ohio, safe for that figurative middle-aged Middle America machinist and his wife. And also to keep Santa Clara County, California, safe for the next generation of computers and the next generation of silicon chips.

If it is a strategy, it is neither an electoral calculus nor a partisan design. On the contrary, my intention is to outline a workable *bipartisan* "industrial" or "competitiveness" strategy for American business.

Of course, those offering competitiveness agendas have to know what they're doing in political terms—what people, politicians and interest groups are willing to accept and what they will reject. Unfortunately, many of the theorists who have waded into the debate with panicky prescriptions for American imitation of Japanese management or heavy-handed transformation of the U.S. economy have ignored this simple reality. But realistic politics means realistic limitations: no panaceas are available.

The proposals I advocate in this book generally originate in the business community.* Nevertheless, their arrangement and packag-

*That is not true of my proposal to crack down on foreign lobbying in the United States (which has a considerable impact in manipulating and thwarting U.S. trade policy and trade law enforcement). No business groups have offered this corrective, but U.S. Trade Representative William E. Brock agreed with the idea in a January 1984 conversation.

ing are largely mine; moreover, the supporting political and public opinion analysis is entirely mine and cannot be laid at the doorstep of any of the business organizations and corporations whose programmatic ideas are expressed herein. On this subject matter, from a policy standpoint, corporate America is worth listening to. Businessmen may be naïve and ineffective in many areas of politics and national policy, but global competitiveness is not one of them. Many of this country's senior executives have a pretty good idea of what will make this country's high- and low-tech industries more competitive again. American management is hardly the peerless elite it was portrayed to be a decade or so ago, but neither are American executives economic ostriches with their heads in the sand, as portrayed in the literature of two or three years ago. There is, after all, some truth to the old saying that "the business of America is business." The upshot is that the corporate agenda is basically a practical one. Most of what is in this book is widely accepted or reasonably workable within the present confines of politics and ideology. What I have tried to do is to pull it together and give it a political, a historical, an economic and, to a limited degree, even a philosophical framework.

This book does not propound a "national industrial policy" of a far-reaching sort involving industrial redevelopment banks or mechanisms for picking winning or losing industries or technologies. That would mean too much interference in the marketplace. What I do advocate—and what many in the business community similarly urge —can realistically be called an industrial or competitiveness *strategy*. In various conversations over the last few months, I've found that many strong "industrial policy" critics like Commerce Secretary Malcolm Baldrige and National Association of Manufacturers President Alexander Trowbridge are simultaneously proponents of the competitiveness strategy terminology and idea—of the notion that because so many other nations are assisting and subsidizing their own industries to compete in global markets, the U.S. government also must begin taking a more active role to "level the playing field." Du Pont Chairman Edward Jefferson has gone so far as to call this distinction between "strategy" and "policy" absolutely critical. Proindustrial strategy thinking is hardly a very radical view. Actually, if labels are necessary, it's probably a moderate conservative viewpoint (that being the description that would fit the politics of most of its proponents).

Unfortunately, the idea that the United States needs an "industrial strategy" to rebuild global competitiveness is taken by some conservatives as false and a reflection on the adequacy of so-called Reaganomics. There is a bit of truth in the latter observation. Early Reagan policy was caught up in the exaggerated expectation that tax cutting, money supply manipulation and deregulation could revive what was still seen as a stand-alone U.S. economy. Little attention was paid to the global context. But by early 1984, that neglected international economic context had become critical, what with a greatly overvalued dollar, collapsing U.S. trade patterns and a trade deficit accelerating toward $100 billion a year.

Nevertheless, national circumstances argue against partisan quibbling. Democratic critics of the administration, for their part, spent late 1982 and much of 1983 in pursuit of a policy of bringing back agencies similar to those of the 1930s New Deal—a new Reconstruction Finance Corporation and the like—to meet the different global challenge of the 1980s. So the question is not which party or ideology is going to have to update its policies; the question is which will succeed in doing so first (or which will be in power to implement its new perceptions). Government does have a new role, but only a limited one—to be developed with restraint.

As a personal aside, my previous book *Post-Conservative America,* written in late 1981, suggested that first-stage Reaganomics would indeed have to give way to a second stage in which business-government partnership would play a much greater role. For a while, I had planned on amplifying that argument in *Post-Conservative America.* Instead, after a two-year hiatus, I have set forth the argument in this volume. But I think it is more timely as a result.

One hope I have now, and which I would have understated back in 1981, is that real-world disagreement between conservative economics and centrist industrial strategy can be minimized. To be sure, a few libertarian and supply-side economists will balk. Yet if you ask the typical conservative businessman or free-market economist or conservative think-tank official for reaction to the fifteen proposals spelled out in chapter 4 as an industrial strategy, he or she will probably favor nine to twelve of them. In mid-1983, the New Jersey–based Opinion Research Corporation polled corporate executives on whether they favored the "industrial policy" or "free market" approach to economic development. Predictably, 63 percent took the free-market position while just 37 percent embraced the industrial policy side. However—and the point is pivotal—executives pro-claiming their free-market fidelity proved almost as supportive as their proindustrial policy colleagues of a long list of government programs and measures designed to help business compete abroad. All of this is enumerated at considerable length in this volume. Likewise, public opinion polls show Republican and conservative voters equally as supportive of these activities as Democrats and liberals. When I set forth an industrial or competitiveness strategy, it is principally this "emerging consensus" subject matter I'm talking about.

Experts increasingly agree that much of the dislocation of Ameri-can industry over the last three years has stemmed from the impact of macroeconomic policy—huge budget deficits, high interest rates and an overvalued dollar. Industrial policy protagonists, too narrow in their focus, have overexaggerated the purely structural side of U.S. difficulties. A return to "normal" economic circumstances—small budget deficits and a cheaper dollar—would clearly reduce the pres-sures that have backed American industry up against the competitive wall. I do not see how anyone can prescribe a far-reaching industrial policy agenda without weighing this offsetting argument. By con-trast, the theoretical benefits of a better macroeconomic climate detract little from the merits of a commonsense competitiveness agenda. Moreover, theoretical benefits are not necessarily achievable. Over the last decade, budgets, interest rates and currency rates have been as changeable as politics and trading patterns. Just who is going to restore "normal" circumstances? I digress here to indicate that while my thesis embraces the need for a better macroeconomic policy and climate, I hardly intend to try to blueprint it. Macroeconomic policy for the mid-1980s is a separate book—somebody else's book.

Caveats are also in order on the rather cursory approaches I take in three other areas. Let me stake out my frame of reference and my own basic thinking on each.

On nationalism: This volume more or less endorses what amounts to a new "economic nationalism" for the United States. The term is less than ideal, and I use it with some reluctance because of its pejorative connotation in many quarters. The Reagan administration —U.S. Ambassador to the United Nations Jeane Kirkpatrick, in particular—has also argued that we are seeing a new nationalism abroad in the land. My own slightly different analysis is that across a wide spectrum of values—economic, ethnic, biological, racial and regional—the last several decades have seen a parochialization of loyalties not just in the United States but in the world. As part of this larger pattern, economic outlooks and commitments have been Balkanizing. Countries and states and cities and ethnic groups seek to take care of themselves before they take care of others. It's not the first time. History records other similar patterns in previous eras of great social and economic upheaval—during the Reformation and the rise of capitalism, then again during the nineteenth-century industrial revolution. In such periods, nations that don't make self-interest and self-protection their yardsticks can lose ground. In more specific terms, my frequent use of the word "nationalism" to describe assertion of U.S. economic self-interest is borrowed from a definition offered in early 1983 by management philosopher Peter Drucker. He suggested—quite rightly, in my opinion—that it was time to build an awareness of trade and comparative U.S. economic strength into official policy making, and he set forth three options: (1) an "internationalist" model, which simply noted the competitive consequences of U.S. actions; (2) a "nationalist" model, which considered policies with an eye toward strengthening the U.S. competitive position in the world; and (3) a "mercantilist" model, in which bolstering the nation's global trade position became U.S. policy's major objective. Where this book recommends "nationalism," it does so in the sense of the Drucker "nationalist" model (and as opposed to Drucker's two other alternatives).

On U.S.–Japanese relations: This book suggests that the United States must take economic competition with Japan almost as seriously as we take strategic and military competition with Russia. Many other analysts have said the same thing. But I think that the point deserves some preamplification. Japan's success in eroding U.S. trade in a number of high-technology sectors is a definite threat to America's economic future. True, other East Asian countries are beginning to develop some similar skills and world market advantages, in part because of lower wages and in part because (as in Japan) local government and business work in partnership to nurture trade. Japan, however, poses the major challenge—all the more so because Japan is also one of this country's most important allies. Part of what the United States must do—and even the Japanese agree that this is so—is to develop an industrial strategy of our own in tax policy, education, antitrust, research and development and even patent law. At the same time, though, the United States must also push for new guidelines in world trade of a type able to reach and restrict the foreign industrial policy trade subsidies and business-government partnerships that give foreign goods advantages over ours and that are uncontrollable under present law. Negotiating those rules will not be easy. And in the meantime, our own trade laws must be changed. The likelihood is that this will generate considerable conflict with Japan and other U.S. allies—and if so, better that than the stress of U.S. economic erosion. Relative to our present economic circumstances, the United States is trying to defend too much of the world—to uphold the Pax Americana rooted in the very different economic circumstances of the late 1940s and the 1950s. If we cannot negotiate new trade and economic relationships, these obsolescent strategic arrangements may rupture before they, too, can be modified. Public frustration is great. Before too much longer, U.S. public opinion is likely to say: either bring home the (trade) bacon or bring home the U.S. troops.

Someone could usefully write a book on "United States–Japanese Strategic Relationships in an Era of Global Trade Realignment." My own chapters only touch upon points that deserve lengthier, expert analysis. But from my standpoint, at least, it is not "Japan-bashing" to insist on a redistribution of Pacific defense burdens and a redefinition of global trade rules. On the contrary, such measures could turn out to be pivotal to maintaining the Western alliance.

On America's high-technology future: Finally, this book does not elaborate much on the importance of high technology to the economic future of the United States, save to repeatedly acknowledge the prospect. Probably I should stake out from the very beginning my approach to early 1980s "high-tech political romance" as opposed to the future central role of technology and scientific entrepreneurialism in the U.S. economy. Of the latter, I have no doubt. And if this book does not set forth in detail various industry proposals to support research and development and technical education, it is partly because I have little knowledge in those areas. The appropriate subsection of chapter 4 merely reiterates a number of high-tech industry proposals. At the same time, this book is dismissive of the first-wave political economics of high tech—the so-called Atari Democrat notion of targeting a whole string of glamorous industries from robotics to fiber optics as part of a campaign to hurry up history into making the United States one big Silicon Valley. That hype was mounting apace as I began writing these chapters in early and mid-1983. Since then, it seems to have retreated into a more mature realization that Pittsburgh cannot turn into an Appalachian Santa Clara and that the romance of high tech is only a distant political reality. Happily, that leaves us freer to pursue more solid, real-world efforts to encourage technological innovation and development and (most often) implant it in older, basic industries badly in need of competitive retooling.

And will we succeed in "staying on top" with a new competitiveness strategy? I think so. For a while, at least.

KEVIN P. PHILLIPS
Bethesda, Maryland
February 1984

ACKNOWLEDGMENTS

Inasmuch as a fair part of this book is devoted to spelling out the evolving positions of major elements of the U.S. business community on the notion of an "industrial strategy," I am particularly appreciative of my conversations with or assistance from a number of officials and executives of major organizations and corporations: Alexander Trowbridge, president of the National Association of Manufacturers; Arthur Levitt, chairman of the American Business Conference, and Jack Albertine, president; Richard Lesher, president of the U.S. Chamber of Commerce, Jeffrey Joseph, vice-president for domestic policy, and James Morris, director of the U.S. Chamber Survey Research Center; Charls Walker, chairman of the American Council for Capital Formation; Charles McKittrick, Washington vice-president of International Business Machines (for the Business Roundtable Task Force on Industrial Policy); Allan Cors, Washington vice-president of Corning Glass (for the Labor-Industry Coalition for International Trade); and John Meagher, vice-president/government relations for LTV Corporation and chairman of the Basic Industries Coalition. As for senior officials of the Reagan administration, I would like to extend my thanks for conversations with Commerce Secretary Malcolm Baldrige and U.S. Trade Representative Bill Brock. Finally, Opinion Research Corporation, based in Princeton, New Jersey, one of the leading polling firms for U.S. business, was helpful in authorizing use of some of its data. I should add, however, that none of the above bear any responsibility for my interpretations or proposals.

Many of the ideas and theses set forth in this book took their earliest form in my publication, the *Business & Public Affairs Fortnightly*. In this regard, I would like to thank my former and present editorial assistants, Kay Edwards Shlaes and Michelle Moore. At Random House, Inc., my publishers, I owe thanks and appreciation to Jason Epstein, Grant Ujifusa and Derek Johns. And the book would never have been launched or finalized without the help and insights of my agent, Bill Leigh.

Contents

STAYING ON
TOP

Introduction:
A Call to Arms

It is time for the United States of America to begin plotting its economic future, not stumbling into it. Our economy is still number one, but it is mightily threatened by realities we have yet to face and respond to. Only now are we arriving at a painful awareness of how far this country managed to slip during the late 1960s and the 1970s from its accustomed global position.

All of the erosions—economic, institutional and strategic—are related, but this book is about only one: the decline in the international competitiveness of our economy and of many important individual industries. As for analyses and remedies, I want to emphasize the *politics* of staying on top: how much of what we had we can manage to reclaim, where we are openly losing, what we can do instead of what we are now doing, and under what technological, partisan, ideological, regional and interest-group banners we should proceed. I will assert that we do not need a full-fledged national industrial policy, as that term is commonly understood, but that we do need a tough-minded industrial and trade strategy—something I want to spell out and define here.

The United States has been a national Rip Van Winkle, awakening after a twenty-year sleep. The first ten years brought the Vietnam war and an eroding U.S. domestic institutional capacity and international credibility. The second ten brought us Watergate, the pseudopurification of electing a Sunday schoolteacher President, school busing schemes that emptied our cities, naïve global human rights crusades, delay of major energy projects to protect tiny fish and obscure plants, tax theories sketched on cocktail napkins and, finally, a nostalgic denial of the economic role of government. Small wonder we have lost ground—some battles, but not the war—to countries that spent these years devoting themselves to economic productivity, trade and industrial strategy.

The nature of the challenge now seems to be clear. Back in the late 1970s, the American public kidded itself into thinking that energy costs were the central problem of the international economy, with Arabs the burnoosed bogeymen. President Carter went on television in a sweater and proclaimed "the moral equivalent of war" against the Organization of Petroleum Exporting Countries (OPEC). We can now see that the energy crunch of the 1970s was part of a larger crisis: the painful transformation of the world economy from an industrial to a postindustrial mode, from smokestacks to information and high technology.* This massive and global phenomenon, which in its earlier period was the engine of inflationary and energy price upheavals, is now working its way through a later stage: a painful dislocation and geographic shift in world production patterns. High-technology industries are booming in several dozen affluent, well-educated and privileged areas of the United States, but at the same time more and more of what used to be made in Youngstown, Cleveland, Baton Rouge and the Carolina Piedmont is now being manufactured in China, Japan, Mexico and Brazil. As unemployment has soared, the United States and many European countries find that they can no longer afford the expensive welfare entitlements created in the 1960s and 1970s. And while cutbacks in programs have spread, economic nationalism has intensified, as nations take steps to protect their own industries, markets and workers. Moreover, as things now stand, American companies face competition from foreign business-government partnerships—not just from overseas corporations but from working alliances of corporations and government ministries of international trade and industry. So, unlike the presumed crisis posed by energy, a genuine confrontation, with

*For detailed analyses of the related transition of U.S. politics, see my previous books *Mediacracy: American Parties and Politics in the Communications Age* (New York: Doubleday, 1975) and *Post-Conservative America* (New York: Random House, 1982).

the emotional equivalent of war, may now be in the offing for the United States: the challenge of reestablishing our global economic primacy, and doing so in a world very greatly changed from the era of comfortable American trade and industrial leadership that obtained before Vietnam.*

Possibly the world economy will continue to move in directions that undermine the United States. Even now, our sense of failing competitiveness has already produced a set of identifiable political and institutional crises: for business, for labor, for conservatives, for liberals, for economists and diplomats. However, a framework for self-help and self-renewal is also at hand. Across the board, roles, ideas and strategies must be adapted to new circumstances:

- American businessmen, facing foreign competition underwritten by business-government partnerships, must set aside old concepts of laissez-faire and adjust to—even advocate—new kinds of business-government collaboration.
- Labor leaders, accustomed to the Anglo-American tradition of conflict with management, must accept a new kind of cooperation and a commitment to productivity, new technology and product quality. Short of that, the industries that have been organized labor's greatest sources of employment may not be able to survive.
- Political conservatives must accept a new probusiness role for government—from coordination of economic and trade strategies to targeting of export assistance and credits—as a necessity. Without that role, our economic rivals (not least conservative and neomercantilist Japan) will continue to displace American products in domestic and world markets.
- Political liberals must accept that there is little support for bringing back federal agencies based on New Deal models to run the U.S. economy, and that much of the new business-government cooperation will back economic development and nationalist (ex-

*Alarmist as this may seem, consider the remarks of U.S. International Trade Commission Chairman Alfred Eckes to a (Washington) National Press Club audience in September 1983: "Some might describe the emerging [U.S. international trade] relationship as reminiscent of the colonial trade pattern this country had with Great Britain in the eighteenth century. . . . Our trade with East Asia illustrates the pattern. Last year, our five leading exports to Japan were corn, soybeans, wheat, cotton and coal. Our five leading imports from Japan were automobiles, trucks, oil well casing and motorcycles."

port, trade competition) agendas rather than abstractions like so-cial justice or social welfare.

To the man in the street, the dramatic, even frightening, reality of our economic crisis can be summed up in the words "economic war with Japan." This is a second recent attempt to give our problems a devil mask: first OPEC and now Japan. Nevertheless, fear of Japan promises to be an effective spur for domestic economic and political modernization. Theodore White, who is no gloomster, in *America in Search of Itself,* published in 1982, characterized relations between the United States and Japan as an economic combat zone:

> The most precise and coordinated trade war of all time is being waged against American industry under the direction of the Japanese govern-ment. . . . Against such an onslaught directed by a foreign power, no single American corporation, no matter how large, neither General Mo-tors nor U.S. Steel, can stand. The Japanese Minister of International Trade and Industry confronts them with a devastating adversary—a foreign government-industry partnership.[1]

By 1983, that view had caught on so well here that the Japanese began a major campaign to rid themselves of the "Japan, Inc." label. The Japanese government's role is exaggerated, they say with some jus-tification—but with no great effect. In 1982, Midwestern businessmen who organized a Metalworking Fair Trade Coalition to press for import restraints scheduled their first meeting for December 7, the forty-first anniversary of Pearl Harbor. And a 1983 issue of *Business Week* magazine ran an extraordinary warning by the late Bernard Mitchell, one of the few Americans to have served as president of a major Japanese corporation, Pioneer Electronics. According to Mitchell, unless our government abandons outdated rhetoric and ineffective policy rules, "there is no corrective mechanism that can save the Western economies from economic and political collapse." The Japanese, as he portrayed them, are simply too efficiently orga-nized.

> The Japanese system—based on economic power lodged in a cartel of banks, government, and business interests—is one of strong nationalism, excessive discrimination, limited personal freedom, a labor force of will-ing captives, savers who happily demand little as payment for forgoing

current consumption, and shrewd negotiators who demand enormous concessions but grant none in return. Thus, it is capable of producing more goods and services of higher quality and at lower cost than any other nation in the world.[2]

An exaggeration, perhaps. But also a challenge. To the Japanese, if I may paraphrase Von Clausewitz's well-known quotation, business has become a continuation of war by other means. Real military expenditure still accounts for only 1 percent of the Japanese GNP. Under the protection of the U.S. defense umbrella, Japan is currently free to engage in full-scale economic and trade competition. So if the United States during the 1970s was guilty of virtual economic disarmament, one could easily portray the Japanese as practicing samurai economics—striking to destroy the heart of a rival's industrial base.

The United States is now contemplating imitation. Yet in the face of Japan's enormous inroads into U.S. markets and industries—50 percent of the new cars on California roads in 1984 are Toyotas, Datsuns, Hondas and Mazdas—it's extraordinary how many serious U.S. commentators are wasting time and effort debating whether or not Japan has something called an industrial policy and whether or not government involvement and planning have played a major role in Japan's economic ascent. The hairsplitting goes on for high stakes, of course. Each side of the debate here hopes to shape American policy by its interpretation of how Japan succeeds. On one hand, liberals, convinced that government planning and regulation are the key to our economic future, find it useful to argue that the Japanese government in general, and the famous Ministry of International Trade and Industry (MITI) in particular, guided the Japanese economy to its present eminence. Accordingly, liberals can be found urging the creation of a federal economic planning council, a national industrial development bank and the like. To this, conservatives say, wrong again: look at the trend of tax reduction in Japan; look at Tokyo's low cost of raising business capital (less than half our cost); look at the Japanese national commitment to savings, to productivity and to group consensus. Government planning isn't responsible for Japan's success, they claim; MITI made any number of mistakes, and fortunately for Japan, business often, as with Honda and Sony, ignored MITI's advice.

This ideological polarization seems absurd. Rarely has so large a truth lain in the middle of so big a debate. For starters, by all the evidence, liberals are correct when they say that government's role was important as it promoted industrial growth and success during the 1970s not only in Japan but also in Korea, Taiwan, Brazil and a number of other countries whose economic advance during that decade became a byword.

Europe's experience with industrial policy is admittedly mixed. For East Asian nations, however, even William Krist, the Reagan administration's Assistant U.S. Trade Representative for Industrial Policy, acknowledges the industrial policy approach as having proved generally successful.

> Other countries, however, have adopted industrial policies akin to those of Japan and are succeeding in winning a larger share of world export markets. For example, after Japan quadrupled its share of world exports in the 1960s to 11 percent, Taiwan, Korea, Hong Kong and Singapore tripled their share of world exports in the 1970s. Other large industrializing countries, such as Brazil and Mexico, have been guiding their growth though current international indebtedness is complicating their trade growth.[3]

Does it matter if some of that official role came in planning, some in labor or resources allocation, some in targeting subsidies and some in simply establishing (or maintaining) the sort of tax and capital-formation climate that enterprise needs to flourish? Effective tax policy coordination between business and government is no mean achievement in itself. For conservatives here to say that Japan owes little or nothing to official industrial policies—to dismiss the economic coordination and consensus-building achievements of one of the world's longest-enduring conservative regimes—strikes me as an exercise in analytical irrelevance.

At the same time, conservatives seem eminently correct when they argue that much of Japan's success flows not from the sometimes fallible bureaucracy of MITI but from the enterprising and frugal character of Japanese society and from the capitalist economics of Japan's enormously successful ruling Liberal Democratic party, which, despite its name, is very definitely right of center. In practical terms, the managers of Japan, Inc., have used the leverage of government planning and power to promote a generally conservative economic system and set of cultural values. Indeed, one could almost say that government guidance has been effective in part because of

Japan's mildly authoritarian cultural milieu. Progressive academicians prefer to skirt such recognition, that the values of MITI are not those of the Harvard Faculty Club. Yet it's true, and it in turn supports a notable irony: that "industrial policy"—a neomercantilist business-government partnership—has enjoyed its most substantial successes under conservative or right-wing regimes like those found in Japan, Gaullist France, Korea, Brazil and Taiwan. That's probably because such governments have meant business, in both senses of the word. One can conclude that around the world effective, not theoretical, industrial policy fits part and parcel with what can be called de facto business nationalism.

For the rest of the 1980s, the United States, I think, faces a choice of three basic approaches. The first, and the most conservative in ideological terms, consists of simply continuing the market-oriented and thus largely uncoordinated economic approaches put into place by the Reagan administration—ongoing emphasis on tax reduction, business deregulation and curbing the growth of the federal government. Proponents of this view, of course, reject the idea of any increased government role: economic decision making and resource allocation should be left to the marketplace, even if the new marketplace is global.

The second approach, favored by the left and center-left, embraces a major new federal intervention in the economy. Tailored to mirror some of the bolder components of foreign industrial policy, it goes under the same name—industrial policy. Specifics vary from blueprint to blueprint, but prominent among the proposed new government mechanisms advocated are: (1) a federal economic coordinating council or strategy board, empowered to bring together representatives of business, labor and government to establish and pursue national priorities; (2) a national industrial development bank, authorized to fund the restructuring of troubled industries; and (3) a federal technological research agency.

The third alternative, which falls between the two both ideologically and programmatically, can be called a strategy of industrial competitiveness. In recognition of the increasingly political nature of the global marketplace, this approach stresses a new government activism in export promotion and trade policy and a new business-government cooperation, while simultaneously rejecting industrial policy advocates' insistence on new federal economic planning and supervisory agencies. The assumptions governing policy would be those of increased U.S. economic assertiveness around the world, not massive new government intervention at home. Unlike so-called structuralists on the left, competitiveness-strategy advocates would agree with the Keynesian "macroeconomists" that many—although by no means all—of our industrial difficulties of the early 1980s were greatly aggravated by economic policy dislocations: huge budget deficits, high interest rates, an overvalued dollar.

In present circumstances, the third option is the centrist position. Many prominent Democratic business leaders, economists and officials of previous administrations have implicitly embraced it by rejecting the positions held by industrial policy advocates as untested and too extreme.* And during 1983 and 1984, business, Republican and conservative support has grown for many of the positions regarding the kind of agenda for competitiveness I am about to set forth, and there has been a distinct if not openly acknowledged movement away from the laissez-faire attitude that prevailed during 1981 and 1982. This book, of course, attempts to present a comprehensive political and political-economic case for the third approach.

The rebuttal to an industrial policy, as commonly perceived, is both political and economic. Given a moderately resilient national economy, the realities of U.S. governance—from our town-meeting, Jeffersonian political heritage to our fifty-state crazy quilt of business-development subsidies and practices—work against close replication of a MITI or establishment of new federal agencies designed to enthrone federal officials as the arbiters of which industries wax and which wane. Foreign-type industrial masterminding is not all

*In this regard, it's probably useful to cite the 1983 comments of three leading Democrats who head national business organizations: Arthur Levitt, chairman of the American Stock Exchange; Alexander Trowbridge, president of the National Association of Manufacturers; and John Albertine, president of the American Business Conference. In a *Harvard Business Review* article, Levitt argued that "An industrial policy of control that tinkers with the delicate, infinitely complex mechanism of the free market or attempts to shunt the flow of capital and resources into areas of perceived need will be doomed to failure." Albertine has indicated that "an industrial policy wouldn't work because it would degenerate into raw politics," while Trowbridge has said, "Proposals for intervention by the federal government in sectors and specific industries simply assume a wisdom on the part of those in the public service that nobody can take for granted." (These comments came in conversations with the author.)

Leading Democratic economists like former Council of Economic Advisers Chairman Walter Heller and former Budget Director Charles Schultze have also been critical. Unless and until these views change, proposals for ambitious federal planning and economic intervention mechanisms will not be able to muster a consensus within the Democratic party, to say nothing of Congress or the country.

that compelling, either. To be sure, some foreign practices involve powerful planning agencies, but these are a minority. And those with a record of enviable successes are even fewer. By contrast, a number of the less interventionist elements of industrial policy can be found in many Western nations—attitudes and institutional arrangements that give a nation's industries and exporters a global competitive advantage and therefore merit our analysis and in some cases our adoption of them. It's easy to list a number of these approaches our competitors use and we do not: first, government coordination of industrial competitiveness and trade objectives; second, official commitment to upholding national economic interests by taking full advantage of existing international trade law—either in loopholes or opportunities to restrict the unfair practices of competitors; third, active government assurance of export credits, subsidies and loans to ensure that a nation's industries are fully competitive with foreign competitors similarly favored; fourth, a greater sense of cooperation —of a shared national economic stake—among business, government and organized labor. Some of these approaches represent techniques and attitudes the United States is going to have to embrace.

To move beyond the pointless debate over whether it is foreign industrial policies or some other elusive approach that has undercut the competitive position of U.S. industries, consider these five illustrations of how foreign corporations, aided by government, can outsell their American rivals, often even in our own market.

Capital costs: A Japanese company raises money by getting bank loans with interest currently pegged by the government near 7 percent; a Korean company raises money by getting the 6-percent loans available for production of exports; an American company typically has to pay 12 or 13 percent for its capital.

Tax breaks: An American company pays essentially the same federal taxes in domestically manufacturing goods for sale in Calcutta as it would for sale in Connecticut; a Korean company avoids taxes in the manner described by Shuh Eun Suk, executive vice-president of Daewoo Heavy Industries: "When we export, we don't pay any income tax, we don't pay the defense tax, and we don't pay tariffs on the imported raw materials that go into the exports. That adds up to almost 40 percent of the production cost."

Product exclusion by government monopolies: U.S. cigarettes are the most competitive in the world—the best and the cheapest—

and Japan's cigarette market is the second largest in the free world. But American manufacturers have only 1.7 percent of the Japanese market. Although minor reforms are under way, the official Japanese Tobacco and Salt government monopoly has set prices so that American brands cost 40 to 50 percent more than the Japanese brands. A Japan-based company can sell tobacco in the monopoly; an American-based company effectively cannot.

Resource subsidies: A company in Mexico, Africa or the Middle East produces petrochemicals with the help of natural gas furnished free or at minimal cost by the government, because in many oil-producing countries natural gas is simply flared off. A company in the United States has to buy its own natural gas, and with feedstocks (like natural gas) accounting for nearly half of the cost of running a petrochemical plant, the American firm cannot produce at competitive prices.

Antitrust: Two steel-manufacturing concerns in nations belonging to the European community get together under Common Market and individual government aegis to exchange plants and specialties so that each can survive by targeting only one or two segments of the deteriorating steel market; two similar concerns in the United States would violate U.S. antitrust laws if they practiced the kind of collusion found in Europe.

That such ideas, approaches and arrangements are widespread among our major Free World trading partners is indisputable. So is the lack of effective countermobilization on the part of the United States. Table 3 in chapter 1 shows the enormous gap between what other countries do to promote enterprise and exports and what the United States does. The disparity has become crippling. It is this dimension of foreign practice—and not the notion of heavy-handed government direction of industry—that U.S. policy makers must begin to embrace.

Shaping a more activist U.S. policy to increase business-government collaboration strikes me as a matter more of common sense than ideology. Nor would this kind of industrial strategy—unlike the central planning ambitions of left-of-center industrial policy proponents—undermine parallel emphasis on revised fiscal and monetary policy. So if I had to come up with a phrase to describe the program, it would not be "industrial policy" but "business nationalism"—a strategy for industrial competitiveness.

Chapter 3 lays out some of the business and university establishments' ideas, and chapter 4 examines fifteen specific proposals in some detail. But let me summarize what makes sense to me as a politically workable centrist program.

Trade Law and Enforcement

1. Establishment of a competition-minded federal Department of International Trade and Industry, whose job will be to foster U.S. competitiveness.
2. Enactment of trade reciprocity legislation.
3. Fuller enforcement of existing U.S. trade laws.
4. Stepped-up federal monitoring and analysis of foreign national industrial policies.
5. Revision of U.S. trade laws to cover aspects of foreign industrial policies.
6. Revision of U.S. antitrust policy to allow U.S. corporations to collaborate on research and technology to meet foreign competition.
7. Expansion of charter and lending activities of the U.S. Export-Import Bank.

Lobbying

8. Intensification of U.S. business lobbying overseas, plus more effective regulation of foreign lobbying in the United States.

Tax Policy

9. Appointment of a national commission on trade and taxation to recommend U.S. tax code revisions to spur international competitiveness.

Management-Labor Relations

10. Support for redirection of labor-management relationships, with particular attention to productivity incentives.
11. Consideration of aid for state and local mechanisms for monitoring industrial plant closings.
12. Establishment of a displaced-worker retraining program modeled on veterans' benefits.

Research and Development and Education

13. Increased support of technological research, including creation of a "basic research trust fund."

14. Protection of U.S. technology against patent abuse, theft and espionage.
15. Enactment of a Morrill Act (land-grant college) equivalent for scientific and technical education.

All of these concepts have political or interest-group support. Some enjoy overwhelming public backing. None is esoteric, nothing that requires Zen management expertise or algebraic enumeration. Taken together, however, they would begin to give us a way to fight back. Effective policy making, of course, will require a successful blend of programmatic common sense, constituency clout, and correct public mood-reading to become law.

The terms used can be important. For example, the term "industrial policy" has gotten a bad name because it was associated with notions of excessive government interference in the economy. And my guess is that some readers will deplore the idea of "business nationalism" as too narrow virtually by semantic given. But precisely this kind of handwringing reveals our weakness. Americans are embarrassed by any form of assertion, even as a pragmatic internationalism demands it. The stakes, however, are real. Our economic strength has been atrophying, and unless the United States helps create a framework in which global neomercantilism can be regulated and our own economic interests safeguarded, bitterness over commercial competition could begin to unravel the Western alliance. Strained U.S.–Japanese economic relations could develop into larger disagreements. So could other trade tensions. International economists would do well to ponder the line in Robert Frost's New England verse: "Good fences make good neighbors." Similarly, bad economic fences—based on yesteryear's inadequate guidelines for free trade—are obviously making restless neighbors.

The issue of what makes for a good fence ought to be the key issue in American politics. Yet nobody—Republican or Democrat, liberal or conservative—has so far shaped a viable, coherent strategy. The election debates of 1984, and the ensuing legislative opportunities of 1985, represent a period in which decisions are going to be made for the rest of the century. Serious thinking cannot wait, because negligence and sloth now can greatly add to the woes of the next recession.

The politics of liberal and conservative approaches to the issue of competitiveness are discussed in chapters 5 and 6. But let me try to preview my critique of both camps, beginning with the left. Most of the national industrial policies offered by the left and center-left have failed to come to grips with (1) the pivotal role of capital formation or incentive economics found in successful industrial policies like that pursued by Japan, and (2) the interaction of an emerging world market and an intensifying economic nationalism. Liberals are too often uncomfortable with both realities. In their various industrial Baedekers, center-left spokesmen rarely note the conservative economic policy components of foreign success. Ignored as well is the ethnic, economic and political Balkanization—economic nationalism, in short—unsettling the world since the early 1970s. Nor is the left attuned to the practical political necessities of policy making. Nitty-gritty constituency considerations are skipped over blithely. Few proindustrial policy speeches, articles and position papers ever seem to address the interest-group politics of who's going to be for what—and why. Flawed scripts have been the result. Accordingly, too much left-of-center advocacy has ranged from crude protectionism and New Deal déjà vu to technological romanticism.

The most important set of proposals has come from Northern urban and labor Democrats eager to link trade protectionism with a set of reworked New Deal economic agencies. These advocates are after more than economic renewal of redundant industries, of course. Trying to save autos and steel and rubber is not just an effort to save jobs; it's also an attempt to preserve a political and interest-group structure, which is perfectly understandable. Progressives remember that every Democratic president elected between 1940 and 1960 owed his critical Northern electoral votes to blue-collar voters, to union registrars and organizers, to the ethnic political machines of the old, heavily industrial Northern cities. The term "social protectionism" is used—and by no means unfairly—to describe the group's dedication to preserving union work forces, upholding union wage scales and reelecting the Northern congressional Democratic cadres essential to the success of federal social welfare legislation.

Preservationism or social protectionism won't work. But at the same time, everyone has to remember that no serious policy maker can write off old basic industries like steel. It's impossible politically and socially. And it's poor judgment strategically. The essential point is that heavy industry will have to be restructured and upgraded technologically as part of a larger national strategy by people with larger national goals and interests.

If anything, it's harder to pay serious attention to the high-tech theorists. Unable to abide the grimy realities of Pennsylvania or Carolina mill towns, these people conjure up what columnist Lewis Lapham has described as a vision of "kindly elves at work in far-off modern California. Happy among the avocado trees, the elves spin the golden threads of fiber-optics and mine the jewels of microchips."[4] The realities of job demography are more pedestrian. The real high-tech opportunity is also likely to be rather down-to-earth —retooling and computerization of basic and service industries, not the glamour of space stations, undersea ecosystems or gene-splicing. Catchy nonsense about "demassified" production, work-at-home "electronic cottages," and a "Cognitariat" busy at a range of new knowledge-worker vocations is cruel and deceptive, as is the idea of bureaucrats perched in Washington aeries skillfully targeting and selecting the technologies of the future.

Yet like the New Deal preservationists, the salvation-through-high-tech crowd does represent an important constituency, in this case of the future, not the past. It's important that their views help shape policy, although it's perhaps even more important that they are not the policy makers themselves.

Of course, there are practical center-left industrial policy advocates who urge compromising around a set of ideas acceptable to both high-tech and basic-industry spokesmen, the old-fashioned "something for your constituencies, something for ours": a government economic coordinating council of sorts; increased research-and-development outlays; some kind of government investment bank; a public works program; crash programs to rescue U.S. education. Yet any agreement here almost guarantees that a superficial position will be taken. Deep and broad divisions are at work because the industrial policy debate intensifies cultural, social and economic differences that have bedeviled the Democratic party since the nomination of Hubert Humphrey. *Futuristic production modes* versus *declining production modes. Upper America* versus *Middle and Lower America. Internationalism* versus *protectionism. Atari progressivism* versus *rednecks, white socks and blue-ribbon beer.* Proposals general enough to paper over these divisions, though perhaps able to catalyze discussion, are unlikely to be the stuff of national mobilization. A larger, supra-Democratic input is necessary, and then a national policy synthesis.

Which brings us to the conservatives, whom I hope to prod into action. In recent years, while traditional smokestack, high-tech liberal and futurist proposals have been churned out, right-wing ideologists and politicians have been too busy defending a free global marketplace that more pragmatic senior business executives believe no longer exists. For the most part, the free-marketeers have failed to frame a serious set of counterproposals. In the long run, this cannot be an adequate politics. Insufficient conservative attention to competitiveness strategy could create what the Italians would call an *apertura alla sinistra*—an opening to the left, by which antibusiness forces can trade on the public's nationalism, economic frustration and desire for action to enact more radical measures. And that could come as early as the next recession. In fact, several left-of-center strategists have speculated that if a "radical" program like the Kemp-Roth tax cuts can go from ridicule to enactment within a few years, the left could conceivably enjoy similar success for its own policy positions.

But the fundamental argument against a business-as-usual free-market response to our current economic problems lies in the changing political basis of competition in the global market. It is simply a new game being played. All of the major Western nations have and will continue to have market-driven economies. An honest appraisal of human nature foretells as much, and rival socialist economics— flawed by their naïve view of human motivation—are on the ebb. A market-driven economy is not, however, the same thing as a free-market economy. In the former, government-aided pursuit of markets can sometimes be exceedingly effective. And from Tokyo to Brasilia, a substantial state economic role—sometimes nationalization of industries, but more often now a mix of capitalism and international marketing—is making the old free-market political model less able to stand up to scrutiny. Corporate leaders and business spokesmen seem even more inclined to think out loud about the problem than academicians and professors on the left.

Accordingly, some of what's being said in the corporate community merits early, lengthy citation and underscoring. Amory Houghton, Jr., chairman of Corning Glass and cochairman of the Labor-Industry Coalition for International Trade, put the issue as follows:

National governments abroad are increasingly reluctant to leave their industrial development to the private sector and the operation of the markets. Advanced industrial countries such as France, Japan, and West Germany have targeted a broad range of industries for special treatment toward accelerated development or revitalization, and the advanced developing countries—Korea, Brazil, Taiwan, Mexico—are if anything still more aggressive in planning and targeting industrial development. Industrial policies, related trade policies, and other more general economic policies are coordinated to achieve enlarged industrial capacity. In contrast, the United States has remained virtually alone in pursuing a basically market-determined allocation of resources across a range of industries from steel, apparel, and autos to semiconductors, fiber optics, and computer-controlled machine tools.

The resulting "industrial policy gap" in many industrial sectors has put American industry at a systematic disadvantage—a growing disadvantage in competition for sales not only abroad but also in our own market, the largest and most open in the world.[5]

Bernard J. O'Keefe, chairman of the National Association of Manufacturers, penned the following analysis for the Boston *Globe* in 1983:

With mind-boggling technological advances in transportation, information and communication in the last decade, the economies of the world's nations have become interrelated and interdependent to the point where it is now as convenient and efficient to do business with Brazil, Korea, Sri Lanka or Taiwan as it is with New York, Philadelphia or Chicago. The result has been an unprecedented degree of competition from abroad in automobiles, metals, textiles and appliances.

The United States has been and still is ill-equipped to cope with this competition, which has become a major reason for unemployment and a primary cause of the recession. We are accustomed to the concept of "fortress America" with our huge, homogeneous domestic market and the insulation of the vast oceans that formerly separated us from our competition. We are not only unaccustomed to competition, but we don't know how to cope with it and, in our naivety and ignorance of world affairs, have put impediments of our own in the way of effective competition.[6]

And *Industry Week* magazine offered this 1983 editorial viewpoint:

The once-insulated American economy has not only become part of a global marketplace; because of its size, wealth and openness, it has become the center—the target—of international marketing activity.

Most nations treat their business and industrial sectors as extensions of government policy, supporting them to achieve social, public-welfare and employment goals. That Socialistic manipulation of industrial activity puts U.S. firms, operating independently by private enterprise rules of competition, at a decided economic disadvantage.

Our national response must recognize that fact of international life. The rules being followed in the U.S. today were designed to cope with a domestic industrial game. The game has changed. It's time to revise the rules.[7]

These trends in the world economy are no cause for celebration. For roughly a century and a half, free-market views have been the dominant Anglo-American theology—though hardly an accurate model of economic reality—to our very great reward and profit. The ebb of our theology may signal a larger ebb. Up to now global free trade, for all its periodic abridgements, has rested on the world manufacturing and trade hegemony of Britain and the United States. But basic industry today is shifting into the Brazils, Taiwans and Koreas, while high-tech leadership is up for grabs among the United States, Japan and Europe. It is my assessment that a pluralistic and Balkanized world economy is more conducive to neomercantilism— to the effectiveness of some state intervention and to new forms of economic nationalism—than to the requirements of free trade. Thus our national problem.

Under the circumstances, I will later suggest to conservatives that they draw on an old heritage. In the early days of the new republic, the political allies of the business and commercial classes were the proponents of business-government partnership and activism. Alexander Hamilton's attempt to institute an early national industrial policy—his famous "Report on Manufactures"—was a prime example. But so was the "American System" of Henry Clay, with its emphasis on a combination of protective tariffs and a national system of internal improvements as a way to expand the domestic market. So was the corporatism and nationalism of Daniel Webster. Thereafter, the political outlook of the business community began to change. From the Civil War through the early twentieth century, the captains of industry were in a position to enjoy laissez-faire. Perhaps the pendulum is now about to swing back to the Hamiltonian view.

Presently, conservatives are lucky to be allies of the business community. Organized labor, despite some important individual contri-

butions to the economic policy debate, narrows the scope and appeal
of liberal and Democratic trade and industrial strategy. The unions
involved in the issue tend to represent shrinking basic industries,
while business usually puts together a far more dynamic and fluid set
of interest groups, many on the cutting edge of the information,
technology and service revolutions.

Therein lies the potential. On many other issues over the last two
decades, corporate interests—and their domination of considerable
aspects of Republican party policy—have been a political drag on
conservatism, especially on the attempt to develop a populist appeal
to so-called Middle America. Senior business executives tend to be
parochial about cultural and foreign policy issues and greedy on tax
issues. Business lobbyists are still apologizing for their role in shaping the giveaways found in the 1981 tax act. The competitiveness issue
is almost unique, however, for the application of business community
expertise. What we're talking about, after all, is trying to pin down
the best way to make our industries (or at least as many of them as
possible) successful against foreign competition, which often relies
on an open business-government economic partnership.

In fact, I will make the case that the most useful proposals for a
new U.S. trade and industrial strategy have come from the business
community and from the myriad commissions and task forces
headed by corporate officials, in reports that appeared in 1982 and
1983.

Nor should that be surprising. Corporate America, including the
Fortune 500 and other institutions, represents a mode of production
and a technology sitting between the future hype of high tech and
the unjustifiable "hold back tomorrow" protectionism obvious in
some of labor's more ambitious formulations. Critiques leveled at
U.S. management in the early 1980s have already been outdated—if
they were ever more than half true—by the alacrity with which
corporate leaders have begun urging and implementing new approaches to technology, training and education, management-labor
relations, product quality and international trade law. Accordingly,
a competitiveness agenda built around the thrust of these recommendations can almost automatically enlist the pragmatic segments of
both the high-tech community and the American labor movement.
Reports from task force after task force can be shown to overlap. In
international policy, moreover, U.S. government global assertiveness
on behalf of business is also emerging as a logical middle way be-

tween a free-trading lassitude, which is no longer possible, and protectionism's parochial demand to close our borders to safeguard domestic markets.

The politics of centrism here is not hard to sketch. So-called big-business moderate conservatism and Sun Belt free-marketeering both lend themselves to a national political and economic transition —the first in terms of institutional fluidity and technological accommodation, the second in terms of regional futurism. By contrast, of the major forces at work, organized labor is probably the most protective, geographically and institutionally, of the past, while the Atari Democrats—to use the descriptive term for liberal high-tech advocates coined a few years ago by *The New Yorker*'s Elizabeth Drew—want to hurry up the future in impolitic fashion. If there is to be a vital center in a new political economics, something along the lines of business nationalism should fit the bill.

TABLE I.
Industrial Strategy and Political Dynamics

Pressure for Speed-Up of Economic Future			*Pressure for Protection of Economic Past*
	Political Center of Gravity		
Maximum			Maximum
High-Tech Neo-liberals	Sun Belt Conservatives	Big-Business Moderate Conservatives	Labor Protectionists

Virtually by definition, advocacy of a probusiness competitiveness agenda must fall to conservatives. Currently in the United States and elsewhere in the West, business and nationalist ideologies and constituencies are generally identified with a center-right politics, making it hard to imagine the requisite policies being implemented from any other direction. A center-left industrial approach, meanwhile, would tilt in the direction of economic planning and structural rearrangement of U.S. industry.

Obviously, American center-right politicians and thinkers are a

long way from agreement over either business-government-labor collaboration to promote trade and industry or new federal mechanisms
to combat "unfair" foreign government-business partnerships. Free-
market purists are, of course, highly skeptical about any form of
government activism. But my analysis, amplified in chapters 5 and
6, is that nationalism, in the sense of support for a more aggressive
international posture, should galvanize conservative opinion molders
and electorates.

As for interest groups and public opinion, the basis for enactment
of a program seems essentially in place. Indeed, major elements of
a serious program have already been proposed by business, conservative, Republican and moderate Democratic spokespersons at the
federal, state, trade association and corporate levels. What's lacking
—and what the effort here might help to shape—is an overall center-
right political and ideological foundation for what must be a new
federal government activism on behalf of U.S. industrial competitiveness in a world grown cold and challenging.

CHAPTER
1

The Rust Bowl and the Crisis of American Industry

When proposals for a national industrial policy first began to appear during the late 1970s, they were widely dismissed as straws in the wind from a malaise-stricken Carter administration. For the most part, corporate America was looking elsewhere: to the election of a Republican President in 1980, which happy event would bring about a new set of probusiness and procapital-formation policies. Even the average voter was in the mood for some old-time economic religion.

But by late 1982, when the Reagan program had proved itself only a partial and very painful success, the public and even a sizable element of the business community signaled willingness to take seriously a new "activist" policy of business-government collaboration. The spur was fear of a possible collapse of U.S. smokestack industries, many of them in sudden and apparent dire straits. Academicians set forth the culpability of American management, while Democratic politicians and ideologists began putting forth an array of industrial policy schemes for a new government agency to retool and revitalize the economy. A new debate was joined.

Then came substantial recovery in 1983 in a number of afflicted basic industries. Accordingly, the left's disparagements of American management came to seem less compelling, as did the image of our basic industries as a crumbling array of has-beens. At the same time, the instant transformation of our economy into an extended biomedical-laboratory-cum-computer facility became less plausible and its advocates somewhat less credible. Obviously Ford, Chrysler, U.S. Steel and B. F. Goodrich were tougher than the onslaughts launched by many of their critics. Moreover, as the strength of the U.S. dollar soared, extending a surge begun in 1981, growing attention came to rest on the overvalued dollar—and, beyond that, on federal budget policy —as a major aspect of the U.S. trade crisis. C. Fred Bergsten, director of the Institute for International Economics and Carter's Assistant Secretary of the Treasury for International Affairs, suggested in 1983 that most of the "competitiveness crisis" stemmed from an over-valued currency that made our rivals' goods cheaper while pricing our manufactured goods out of many foreign markets. Nobody could blame that state of affairs on the Harvard Business School.

This brief history of the industrial policy debate is meant to bring out the point that, just as was true with supply-side economics, early industrial policy advocates were more ideological than genuinely remedial. Too much of the left-liberal enthusiasm for a national industrial policy has been linked to a series of political objectives: first to provide an intellectual life raft for the floundering economic poli-cies of the late Carter regime, then to indict Reagan policies of 1981 and 1982, and finally to furnish ideas for the platforms of the leading Democratic presidential contenders in 1984. A further and related weakness of industrial policy schemes lies in their overreaction to the economic problems of 1982 on several related dimensions: (1) misstate-ment of alleged U.S. "deindustrialization"; (2) exaggeration of federal need to promote high tech to replace crumbling basic industries; and (3) insistence on the need for new federal agencies, planning mech-anisms and government aid programs to resuscitate basic industries allegedly at death's door. Draft in haste, revise at leisure.

What's necessary—and what one hopes will soon arrive—is a synthesis of diagnoses and remedies. Even now, most soothsayers are at least partly correct, even if structuralists trump up the need for neo–New Deal economic planning, while international economists overstate the be-all and end-all role of the overvalued dollar and free-market enthusiasts venture close to spiritualism insisting that Japan, Inc., is a myth.* Fortunately, the ebb and flow of the indus-

*As the *Harvard Business Review* (September-October 1983) noted in prefacing a symposium on "The Political Realities of Industrial Policy," the debate is already warped: "As is often the case with politically sensitive issues, however, discussion itself commonly becomes a form of special pleading—experts talking past each other in favor of their own chosen remedies for the nation's economic ills."

trial policy debate and of the business cycle is reshaping positions on all sides, as rough intellectual edges are worn away and half-baked ideas are being exposed as just that.

To a considerable extent, three major stages of the debate provide a useful way to understand the present controversy. At first, in 1982, conservatives were afraid that as the economy took a nose dive, their ability to shape future economic policy was slipping away. This is when the basic liberal position was stated. But then, as business marshaled its own analyses and arguments, its spokesmen began to counter—and rightly—that a large part of the industrial crisis resulted not from industrial obsolescence or an inability to compete, but from the impact of foreign business-government commercial partnerships. More trade nationalism, not more federal intervention in managing the economy, emerged as an alternative solution. Then many economists rose to challenge industrial policy nostrums on another ground—that U.S. troubles could largely be laid at the door of huge budget deficits, towering interest rates and crippling foreign-exchange rates. These are the major alternative positions now contending with one another.

CONSERVATIVES, MANAGEMENT AND THE BIG SCARE OF 1982

To a substantial portion of opinion-molding America, the deserted unlit steel towers of Youngstown, Lackawanna and Gary in late 1982 signaled that the Japanese, French, Germans, Brazilians and Koreans were coming as surely as Paul Revere heralded the British approach two centuries earlier. Even middle-aged Americans still tend to regard steel as the hallmark of real industrial power. So the banking of the furnaces, as American production dropped to just 39 percent of capacity (and as unemployment crossed into double digits), finally thrust the issue of the competitiveness of our economy into national headlines.

For American business, for the new Republican administration and for conservatives in general, the events of late 1982 can be regarded as a big scare. The new administration took office in January 1981 proclaiming that the economy's central problem was too much government interference in the marketplace—too much taxation, too much regulation, too little capital formation and productive investment. Murray Weidenbaum, chairman of the Council of Economic Advisers, expressed the new administration's philosophy: "Don't just stand there. *Undo* something."

In better times, and absent a global economic upheaval, more of the Reagan experiment might have worked. Not a little of what was to be undone was worth undoing. But as of late 1982, as American basic industries continued to lay people off, national skepticism intensified. The administration's 1981 tax cuts had had little impact, having been offset (proponents said suppressed) by high interest rates. Further tax-cut and deregulationist ardor cooled, as conservatives and businessmen began to acknowledge that the problems of the economy were a good deal more complex than they had first thought.

Enter once again, on stage left, the advocates of government-as-savior. As the November 1982 congressional elections approached, Democratic spokesmen labeled the conservative and business agenda a failure, urging in its place a new round of government activism—public works programs, retraining schemes, federal economic planning and loan agencies.

Convinced that U.S. basic industries were about to become casualties of economic history, center-left politicians, economists and pundits split into two camps, each serving very different constituencies. On one hand, legislators connected with labor or with roots in Northern smokestack regions called for a series of government measures—protective trade laws, tax subsidies, new federal loan mechanisms—to safeguard or even restore the *status quo ante* of industries like steel, automobiles and heavy equipment. Meanwhile, the so-called Atari Democrats, mostly younger moderates from suburban high-tech areas, read the crisis as calling for a different solution: federal mechanisms to speed up the transformation of U.S. industry to high-tech, high-value-added production. Because rhetoric was in greater supply than were specific proposals, the gap between the advocates was not always evident. But they did share one common view: conservative old-time religion had failed and government had a new and big role to play.

Nor were political conservatives the only group under fire. Corporate America's credibility was also very suspect. Poll taker and former Democratic activist Louis Harris in September 1981 had cannily anticipated these circumstances. He noted that in 1980 and 1981 the public had displayed an extraordinary willingness to rally behind key business themes, ranging from increased capital investment to high-priority emphasis on productivity. As never before, Harris observed, the public had supported measures—deregulation, tax breaks—to give business what it had sought. Harris estimated, however, that the public had a "short time fuse. . . . If capital investment is not up sharply, if new technology is not being infused, if the budget isn't well on its way to being balanced, then the patience of the American people will be stretched to the breaking point." By autumn 1982 he warned that it was "entirely possible and even probable" that the United States would be facing a "management crisis" with "profound implications for the relationship between business and government for the rest of the century." Public criticism would begin to come down on U.S. business managers for their "short-term, narrow vision, and demand [would] grow for an expansive redefinition of the role of government."[1]

Harris's vision was prophetic. By late 1982, many Democrats embraced the idea of a national industrial policy as a way to criticize American management skills; they urged placing emphasis on human rather than financial capital and rejected the ongoing conservative antiregulation thesis.

Precisely these arguments are central in the rhetoric of prominent industrial policy advocates. Harvard's Robert Reich and MIT's Lester Thurow, for example, are frequent finger-pointers at the American managerial class. Reich, in his book *The Next American Frontier*, published in 1983, says that U.S. corporate tax cuts haven't been notably productive and that Japan's steel industry has flourished despite having paid out more in environmental outlays than American companies.[2] While the individual assertions may be true, Reich's underlying attempt to make scapegoats of management— never unions, never bureaucrats, but *management*—is essentially political: what impugns management elevates interventionism.

Politics is innately self-serving, and if left-liberal industrial policy is no exception, then neither is the conservative economics it seeks to replace. So let us say it once more. The conservative rhetoric of the period between 1978 and 1981 was much overblown as it promised great things from tax cuts, blamed federal regulation for everything but measles, and held out the prospect of great new achievements from applying business methods to government. Read today, some of the old speeches are embarrassing. Alas, liberal industrial policy advocates spent much of 1983 going too far in the other direction; they tried to make scapegoats of U.S. managers for weaknesses generally shared by society—corporate short-range thinking hardly tops that of politicians, labor leaders, money managers and journalists.

They also went overboard doubting the effectiveness of tax incentives and sidestepped pertinent questions about how the sort of federal regulation, or regulators, on display during the late 1970s could possibly orchestrate an industrial revival for the 1980s.

The larger blow to the thesis of an American managerial class so incompetent that government agencies would have to step in—to save basic industry or to assure a U.S. high-tech future or both— came, however, with the unfolding events of 1983. As the economy climbed out of the abyss of late 1982, basic industries like textiles and automobiles rebounded faster than anyone had imagined. National deindustrialization theses, already dubious enough in available statistics, further lost credibility. Table 2 shows the extent of the rebound as of the summer of 1983.

TABLE 2.
More Smoke from the Stacks: Share of Total Capacity Used

	1978–80 peak (%)	Nov. 1982 (%)	July 1983 (%)
Iron and steel	97.5	39.5	60.8
Autos	91.6	46.2	77.3
Nonelectrical machinery	83.1	62.0	66.7
Chemicals	83.6	64.0	69.7
Aluminum	97.9	57.9	65.7
Textiles	91.3	75.2	88.5

SOURCE: Federal Reserve Board.

Part of the resurgence represented the willingness of industry to shut down redundant capacity, to trim low- and mid-level management, and to introduce new technology. Management, in short, proved at least partly capable, even in some of the nation's hardest-pressed industries, of doing what interventionists believed would have to be assigned to bureaucrats. This does not rebut the need for business-government collaboration, but it undermines those who prematurely laid out a case for massive federal intervention.

Coincidentally, the crisis in the Rust Bowl also helped to prompt a searching look at high tech from a number of perspectives. Reflection and analysis have brought into question both the insistence that the federal government target the emergent technologies for development and the belief that high-tech employment opportunities could begin to handle the human casualties of massive basic-industry shut-downs. In data published in 1983, economist Robert Lawrence of the Brookings Institution suggests that between 1973 and 1979, the latest dates for which statistics were available, the expansion of jobs in high-growth industry rose more in the United States (8.9 percent) than in Japan (6.8 percent) or in Germany (4.9 percent).[3] Numbers like those don't exactly make the case for involving government in high-tech decision making and possibly smothering our innovative capacities in the process. Meanwhile, despite the increases of the last decade, it's also clear that high tech can employ only a handful of workers relative to the payrolls of basic industry, and that plans for an imminent, federally orchestrated switch from the latter to the former are implausible as a matter of demographics as well as of economics and politics.

Accordingly, left-liberal industrial policy advocates suffered from having been too fast off the mark trying to take political advantage of national economic apprehension in 1982, the premise here being that American basic industry was on the brink of collapse absent substantial government intervention. An improved economy makes the national industrial redevelopment banks and economic coordinating councils now seem entirely too bureaucratic. And in the meantime, business and economists alike have developed several other convincing arguments against large-scale intervention in the economy.

BUSINESS-GOVERNMENT PARTNERSHIP AND COMMERCIAL NATIONALISM

In early 1983, press attention tended to concentrate on an interventionist superstructure that glorified high tech, economic strategy boards and national industrial development banks. Hardly anyone bothered to report the detailed exposition by business organizations of the impact of foreign business-government collaboration or their convincing enumeration of proposed trade law and trade policy remedies.

Public boredom thresholds, not bias, were no doubt the reason why we didn't hear more about what the business community thought. But the reportorial omission did camouflage a fundamental weakness of the industrial policy advocates. To them, foreign economic nationalism is acknowledged (and rarely under that name) mainly to show that because our rivals have erected major industrial planning agencies, so must we. All roads lead to the Rome of a bold new federal intervention to plan and manage the U.S. economy. Which is not necessarily the best logic of the matter. Corporate executives and business organizations, by contrast, have looked at foreign industrial policies and perceived a need for moderate nationalist rather than interventionist remedies. If foreign governments aid local industries to the limit and take full advantage of existing trade laws, so must the United States. If foreign governments target assistance and subsidies to their export industries to an extent so extreme that it arguably constitutes unfair trade, the United States must measure that impact and penalize those exports accordingly. If foreign regimes put government and business into partnership via industrial policies, the United States must try to build a new trade law framework to define what's permissible and to restrain what's not.

In 1983, when the Labor-Industry Coalition for International Trade (LICIT), consisting of ten unions and eight major corporations (Corning Glass, Bethlehem Steel, Weyerhaeuser, W. R. Grace, Westinghouse, St. Joe Minerals, B. F. Goodrich and Ingersoll-Rand), published a detailed analysis of our competitiveness difficulties in key industries, its recommendations were essentially along assertive nationalist rather than interventionist lines.* Politicized neomercantilist foreign approaches to both basic and high-tech industries were documented.[4] So was the existence of a major gap between U.S. government help to U.S. companies and the assistance given to foreign corporations by their respective governments, as detailed in table 3. Yet the remedies sought were not federal mechanisms for picking industrial winners and losers but, rather, a series of new approaches to tougher trade policy and trade law enforcement, combined with federal assistance to help our industries meet competition in the new global market. Similar preferences, nationalist not interventionist, have been spelled out in statements and proposals by the Committee for International Trade Equity (CITE)

---

*The Labor-Industry Coalition for International Trade was organized in 1980 by major basic-industry companies and unions to study the international economic issues that affect U.S. business and workers—in other words, the competitiveness problem. Its findings will be quoted with some frequency in this book, partly because of their merit as research, but also because of their significance as a forecast of the areas of competitiveness agenda agreement between the Fortune 500 and the AFL-CIO.

TABLE 3.

The Industrial Policy Gap: Government Assistance for Targeted Industries in the United States and Other Countries

	Other Countries*	United States
Financial and Fiscal		
1. direct or explicit subsidies	+	−
2. soft financing (at lower interest and longer term than market), loan guarantees and open lines of credit	+	o
3. tax and other fiscal measures	+	o
Government Ownership and Discriminatory Procurement		
4. direct government participation (state-owned enterprises, official equity participation)	+	−
5. discriminatory procurement (government procurement or private industry associations)	+	o
Technology Development and Technology Transfer		
6. technical assistance, training and academic or industry research programs	+	o
7. direct government support for commercial research and development	+	**
8. forced disclosure or sharing of technology as condition of market access for foreign companies	+	−
Trade and Investment Policy		
9. requirements concerning foreign investment (co-production requirements, export quotas or import substitution requirements)	+	−
10. trade policy measures (import restrictions, export incentives or subsidies, officially subsidized export credits)	+	o
Industry, Worker and Community Adjustment Programs		
11. industry restructuring or rationalization assistance	+***	−
12. worker adjustment, retraining and relocation assistance	+***	o
13. community adjustment assistance	o	−
Administrative Actions		
14. government, industry, labor cooperative efforts and coordinating activities	+	−
15. industrial organization measures (R&D cartels, production and export cartels, rationalization measures, etc.)	+	−

+ = commonly used
− = not used
o = seldom used
*The other countries represent France, West Germany, Japan, Brazil and South Korea.
**Except for agriculture.
***Primarily in the developed countries.

SOURCE: *International Trade, Industrial Policies and the Future of American Industry* (Washington, D.C.: Labor-Industry Coalition for International Trade, 1983), p. 11.

(an electronics-keyed group), the high-tech Semiconductor Industry Association and others. These proposals will be detailed later, but for the moment suffice it to say that this focus on international competitiveness remedies represents an important element of a moderate alternative to a full-fledged industrial policy approach.

No serious analyst can dispute the serious politicizing of foreign approaches to trade and to both basic and high-tech industries. The issue is whether our own response should be a centrist, business nationalist one—an attempt, as it were, to partially level the global playing field—or a more revolutionary approach, requiring large-scale federal intervention in industrial management and in establishing and enforcing priorities.

Basic Industries

Foreign government involvement is the critical factor. Because of growing global market dislocations, basic industry has been politicized almost everywhere in the West for a simple reason: nations that possess basic industries are loath to let them die; nations that don't have them want to develop them. As summed up by LICIT,

> the governments of Japan, France and West Germany . . . have targeted a broad range of future growth industries for accelerated development and export growth and have also implemented programs to strengthen and improve the competitiveness of their older industries like *textiles and apparel, steel and automobiles* [italics added]. . . . This pattern of government orchestration of industrial development is being emulated by the governments of Brazil, Mexico, Korea and other newly industrializing countries. Targeted for special development and export support are [basic industries] as well as specialized segments of newer growth industries such as computer-peripherals, mini-computers, pharmaceutical products and commuter aircraft.[5]

With political constituencies scripting the fate of older industries here and abroad, free markets are beginning to seem irrelevant. The American steel industry, for one, confronts a situation in which (1) developing nations are subsidizing local steel production to achieve low wage cost inroads into foreign markets and (2) developed nations are subsidizing steel production and exports for reasons based on unemployment, prestige or national defense. The Department of Commerce recently determined that steel producers in Belgium,

France, Italy and the United Kingdom were receiving subsidies equivalent to 13–26 percent of the value of their output. And the Japanese steel industry, with government assistance, has developed an installed capacity twice the size needed to meet domestic needs. The result is a tremendous pressure to retain capacity by exporting, even at prices that cover only variable costs.

In Germany, where steelworkers are about as well paid as in the United States, officials claim that, while local industry could compete against any other producers in cost effectiveness, they cannot compete with taxpayers of other European nations who subsidize steelmakers by as much as $60 a ton. Willy Korf, president of the European Independent Steelworkers Association, has contended that "roughly seventy percent of all European steel enterprises, particularly those in Great Britain, France, Belgium, Luxembourg and Italy, are either nationalized or financially dependent on the state."[6]

To Donald Trautlein, chairman of Bethlehem Steel, the situation as of early 1983 had become a disaster.

> Foreign competitors have formulated deliberate, government-aided strategies aimed at penetration of the U.S. marketplace—irrespective of the financial losses that would be incurred or the response by American steel producers. Their strategies have been predicated on confidence that the U.S. government was not disposed to take firm and effective trade actions.
>
> The results speak for themselves. American steel producers have not had the funds or the growing markets to support investment in a broad range of world-class facilities. Foreign producers, despite large and continuing financial losses, have continued to gain shares in the U.S. market. There is no free-market defense to these policies of other nations.[7]

By mid-1983, when the government announced new U.S. import restraints on specialty steel, U.S. Trade Representative William Brock acknowledged the same political reality: "There is virtually no free-trading in world steel," and there is "an enormous amount of cartelization and subsidization."[8]

The same interest-group and electoral realities that apply abroad apply here. To an extent, the federal government must become the partner and ally of the U.S. steel industry, helping it through a structural crisis. A major shrinkage is inevitable, by 30 or even 40 percent of 1983 capacity. Yet revitalization based on the introduction of new technology is clearly possible, and because the United States cannot sacrifice steel—any more than can France or Germany or Japan—the only question about aid to the industry is what form it will take. Will trade and antitrust be the focus, or will the plight of steel help prompt a larger federal role in this and many other basic industries?

Federal involvement has also been increasing in U.S. automobile manufacturing. Here, too, however, the West is up against a geographic shift of manufacturing and the legacy of an industrial policy that helped develop the Japanese automobile industry to the point where European nations have had to close off their markets. France has held the Japanese share at 2.5 percent, Germany at 10 percent, and Italy at only 0.02 percent. A voluntary agreement limits Japan's share of the British auto market to no more than 11 percent, while a similar agreement limits Japan's exports to the United States. To a considerable extent, world auto markets, like those in steel, are not free markets but politically negotiated markets.

Small wonder that Marina Whitman, chief economist of General Motors and member of Gerald Ford's Council of Economic Advisers, said not long ago that "most observers believe that patterns of automotive production, trade and investment will in the future be determined at least as much by government policies—including so-called industrial policy and the regulatory environment as well as explicit trade policy—as by trends in comparative advantage *per se*."[9]

Textiles are the third old-line sector where U.S. firms face Asian national industrial policies. In a speech in April 1983 to the American Textile Manufacturers Institute, outgoing ATMI Chairman William Klopman, also the chairman of textile giant Burlington Industries, warned that the industry was faced with "aggressive national strategies for industrial development" on the part of China, Japan and Korea.[10] At the time, imports accounted for 30 percent of the apparel sold in the United States, with economists predicting that the figure could reach 50 percent by the late 1980s. Expressing textile makers' fear of inundation by a flood of exports from the People's Republic of China, Klopman told ATMI that "a hint of China's plans for the apparel industry can be seen in the 14 million sewing machines they plan to produce in 1985, up 82 percent from 1980."[11] Further escalation of the attempt to protect U.S. textiles seems very likely.

My intention here is to lay out the politics of a U.S. industrial strategy, not to harp on trade statistics. A critical policy perspective does, however, seem to leap out of the data, speeches and citations: because it is against a nation's survival instincts to allow its basic industries to crumble, and because so many other countries have developed strategic policies to nurture their steel, auto and textile industries through what could be a disastrous period of adjustment, the United States must do the same. Otherwise the U.S. market could become a global dumping ground.

In these sectors, the debate clearly favors a limited industrial strategy over a major interventionist industrial policy, because to most manufacturers the moderate market-oriented approach seems best. Steel, however, is the industry, even by the admission of senior executives, in which the interventionist approach of empowering a federal agency or development bank to suspend antitrust prohibitions and then to restructure and refinance industrial operations has considerable support. Stricter U.S. trade law enforcement here is not enough.

High-Tech Industries

Contrary to the technological utopianism of some futurists, economic nationalism—the call for an assertive U.S. global business strategy—is widespread among high-tech and electronics companies, as well as among old-line heavy industry.

If anything, the foreign business-government high-tech challenge is even more open and robust. In 1982, the French embassy in Washington put out a press release that should be pondered by every American, especially by believers in the illusion of the unassisted marketplace. "The French government," the announcement said, "has approved a five-year plan to invest 140 billion francs, or nearly $20 billion, to place the nation's electronics industry on a technological par with those of the United States and Japan. The investment program . . . will be financed jointly by the state and French industry. The government hopes the program will create 80,000 jobs in France by 1986 and raise the annual growth rate from three percent to nine percent."[12]

In late winter 1983–84, researchers at Los Alamos and at Livermore National Laboratories reported that two Japanese firms, Fujitsu and Hitachi, had moved ahead of the United States in building high-speed computers. The few U.S. companies making super-

computers—the so-called fifth generation of computers—are probably at a competitive disadvantage against Japan's aggressive, govern-
ment-backed effort, warned Los Alamos official William Spack. Yet
if the Japanese take over the world market, he said, the U.S. government and industry would become reliant on foreign technology in the
field.[13]

Meanwhile, a study by Arthur D. Little (Japan), Inc., suggests
that optoelectronics—a fiber-optic–based communications system—
could be the field in which Japan will score its next major market
success. Led by (government-owned) Nippon Telegraph & Tele-
phone Public Corporation's plan to develop an integrated digital
communications network, Japan will pour between $10 billion and
$15 billion into its optoelectronic industry during the next decade.[14]

There could be no clearer warning—U.S. high-tech companies are
up against a lot more than individual foreign corporate rivals. While
the governments of France, West Germany, Japan and other countries are serious about using subsidies funded by taxpayers to develop
coordinate industrial policies to restructure, strengthen or rational-
ize basic industries, that commitment pales beside their dedication
to target government assistance on future high-value-added growth
industries. Listed below are the individual future growth industries
targeted for help by our major competitors: West Germany, France
and Japan.

West Germany
commercial aircraft and
   aerospace computers
computers
electronics, including
   semiconductors

machine tools
nuclear power and other
   alternative energy technologies
telecommunications

France
biotechnology
commercial aircraft and
   aerospace
computers and office machines
consumer electronics
heavy engineering and
   construction projects,
   including
   overseas contracts for

construction of airports,
   subway systems and ports
machine tools and robotics
marine technologies
microelectronics and
   semiconductors
nuclear power and other
   alternative energy sources
telecommunications

Japan

biotechnology	nuclear power and other
commercial aircraft	alternative energy technologies
computers and business machines	telecommunications and
electronics and semiconductors	optoelectronics[15]
machine tools and robotics	

For all practical purposes, this list amounts to a roster of parallel U.S. industries that have justifiable cause for concern. In most of the sectors targeted, U.S. companies' share of world markets has already begun to decline, in some cases quite sharply.

Managers of foreign industrial policies have been candid enough in characterizing their approach. Sozaburo Okamatsu, director of the electronics policy division of MITI, acknowledged that "the basic thinking underlying government policy for the promotion of a specific industry is to extend a helping hand on areas which cannot be accomplished by market mechanisms alone."[16] And a recent Semiconductor Industry Association study on *The Effect of Japanese Government Targeting on World Semiconductor Competition* cited advertising copy placed by Japanese firms in *Scientific American* (October 1980). "Protection," the advertisement read, "has been provided those industries that are in need of protection because of their fragility as emerging industries. Thus protection is negotiated for the semiconductor and computer industries, and telecommunications. . . . Sectors of high value-added, with high growth potential, are afforded as much protection as can be arranged."[17] As of 1983, Japanese officials began to cite a lessened government role, but U.S. competitors are skeptical, believing that the essential system is in place and operating well.*

*In some respects, the debate over whether Japan is cutting back its old industrial policy approach is as pointless as the earlier debate as to whether industrial policy was responsible for the Japanese miracle. The essence of Japan's economic success, however it be described, has come from the country's cultural amenability to teamwork, sacrifice, saving and business-government collaboration. And that collaboration is still in place. In a May 1983 New York *Times* series on Japan's elite trade ministry, Sandanori Yamanaka, Minister of International Trade and Industry, is quoted saying "MITI works in an indirect fashion. When it guides industry, it is with soft hands. It has no real coercive power anymore. The main player is private industry." Toshihiko Tanabe, director of MITI's industrial structure division, added that "MITI is now a kind of co-pilot. At some very critical point, when the risk is very high in new industries, or for the adjustment of ailing industries, government support is sometimes required and business and government must cooperate. To harmonize these actions is the reason MITI exists." And in a similar May 1983 multipart study by the Los Angeles *Times,* Shigenori Hamada, the "godfather" of

As I will later show, the computer, semiconductor, machine tool, electronics and other high-tech industries, though upset, are not looking for new government bureaucracies like MITI to tell them what technologies to pursue and to control their access to capital.* The American record of technological achievement depends too much on innovation to court that kind of interference. Instead, the problems industry strategists concern themselves with are essentially ones of capital formation and unfair competition, and the major remedies advocated are fiscal and nationalist—tax and trade law–related. High-tech spokespeople are furious about official U.S. inaction against foreign industrial policies and want our government to behave like an ally, not a bystander. A Washington commitment to "leveling the playing field" is at least as important to high-tech sectors targeted by foreign governments as it is to basic industry.

From the standpoint of the U.S. trade balance, moreover, assistance for high-tech exports becomes an even greater priority. For national security reasons, the United States cannot surrender a major capacity in steel or machine tools. But the fundamental future of U.S. world trade very clearly lies with high-technology exports, as figures 1 and 2 illustrate. And the data for 1983–84 are not expected to be reassuring. If we cannot maintain our global trade preeminence in high-technology exports, the American economy is in great trouble.

This book displays considerable skepticism toward the so-called Atari Democrat or neoliberal position that the United States can "disinvest" in basic industries and skip off to what cynics call "high-tech heaven." That is simply not a realistic politics or strategy. But our commitment to high technology on another dimension—upgrading U.S. education, focusing on capital availability, improving federal tax treatment of research and development, and curbing foreign industrial policies, preferences and other obstacles to U.S. sales—deserves preeminent national attention.

Japanese electronics and current head of the Japanese Electronics Council, explained that favorable national business response to government guidance lies in a tradition dating back to the country's feudal era: "It is the national characteristic of the Japanese people for the government to play the role of taking initiatives."

*Atari Corporation founder Nolan Bushnell has joked: "I guarantee you that no government agency can target the right industry; in fact, I'll almost guarantee they'll target the wrong one. The targeting role belongs to the entrepreneurs. The problem is that those Atari Democrats would never have targeted Atari."

FIGURE I.

*U.S. Trade Balances with Foreign Nations
in High-Technology and Low-Technology Products, 1960–79*

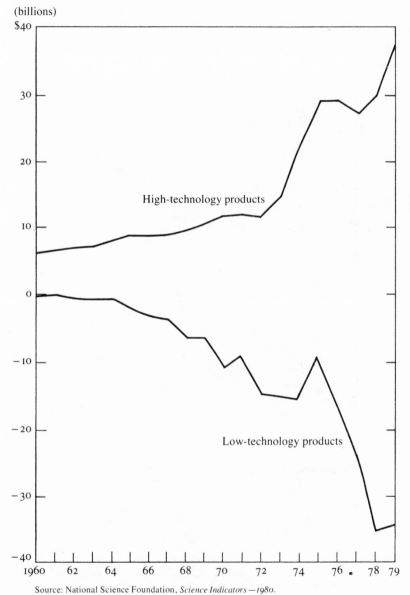

Source: National Science Foundation, *Science Indicators—1980.*

FIGURE 2.
*U.S. Trade Balances with Foreign Nations
in High-Technology Products, 1966–79*

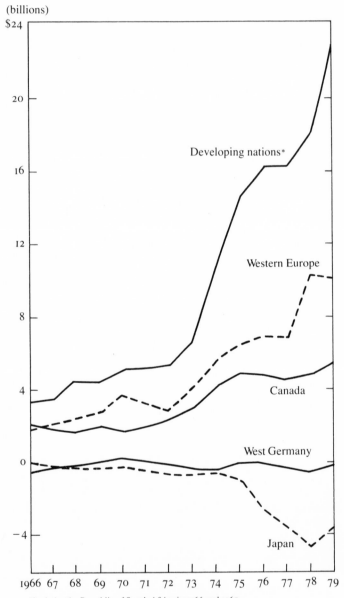

*Includes the Republic of South Africa in 1966 and 1967.
Source: National Science Foundation, *Science Indicators—1980*.

Service Industries

Assistance from Washington is also being sought by the service industries—from banking to transportation, accounting and law—a sector that has been producing a large annual trade surplus. Federal authorities, these industries' spokespeople assert, have no current survey of what U.S. services are being sold (or barred) where. They want one, and have also asked Congress and the administration to develop a stronger trade law and policy, as well as a workable international plan to protect and promote U.S. and international trade in the service area.[18] Awareness is growing that U.S. service exports are coming under increasing world pressure, and that yet another trade crisis may be in the making. A major survey by *Business Week* in March 1984 observed: "From boardrooms in Frankfurt, London and Tokyo to gritty warehouses in São Paulo, tough new foes are elbowing into the market for business and personal services. Already, trade specialists are identifying American services—including travel, tourism, aviation and leisure pursuits—that they say resemble the U.S.'s declining smokestack industries."[19] Chapter 3 will amplify the growing demand for aggressive and reciprocal trade postures from chief executive officers in U.S. service industries.

Let us acknowledge that each and every U.S. industry group is unlikely to benefit from an across-the-board push for a tougher and more aggressive trade posture. Too vigorous promotion of basic-industry objections to foreign industrial policies, for example, could prompt other governments to retaliate by increasing barriers to U.S. service industries. Nevertheless, plenty of room exists for a more assertive U.S. approach to global trade, and from an overall standpoint, business has been making a powerful and consistent case for a combination of stricter trade law enforcement, coordination of U.S. trade strategy, and attempts to rein in foreign industrial policy as a moderate nationalist alternative to left-liberal industrial policy design.

IMPROVED FISCAL AND MONETARY POLICY AS AN ARGUMENT AGAINST INDUSTRIAL POLICY

Yet another growing aspect of the current policy debate has been widespread documentation—which undercuts positions taken by advocates of a full-scale industrial policy—of the extent to which U.S. competitive problems have been generated by the larger difficulties of the economy. By this account, we haven't experienced any serious deindustrialization or any notable failing of the United States relative to Japan. There has been, instead, inept American economic policy making.

So, we can take care of our problems if the United States can cure budget, tax and monetary policies. That will be enough. No controversial mechanisms for the structural relief and rearrangement of industry need be embraced. If macroeconomic policy improves, troubled industries can retool or slowly give way to the movement of history, because market forces are for the most part gradual. This is the antistructural argument.

Francis M. Bator, professor of political economy at Harvard, argues that "a lot of the secular problems people are talking about are really just symptoms of very deep business cycle problems. If we fixed macroeconomics properly, all these structural problems would drop down to third order of magnitude problems."[20] Former Budget Director Charles Schultze has called industrial policy "a solution in search of a problem,"[21] and Yale economist and Nobel Laureate James Tobin has cited a temptation "to misidentify problems today as the result of change" in the nation's economic structure "rather than lay them at the feet of poor macro-economic policy."[22] Tobin suggested that "a lot of the motivation for industrial policy won't be there if monetary and fiscal policy do their job."

At least part of the contention here seems indisputable. There's no doubt many of the problems faced by our troubled basic industries have been magnified two- or threefold by U.S. macroeconomic policy of the late 1970s and early 1980s. Loose fiscal policy and tight monetary policy—high budget deficits and high interest rates—have clearly aggravated our competitive difficulties. As one study noted, in 1980, before the dollar soared against the value of the West German mark, German manufacturers' labor costs exceeded those of the United States by 24 percent; by 1982, the strong dollar had pushed U.S. costs 12 percent above the German.[23]

In industry after industry, corporate executives have cited the overly strong dollar as having devastated our export market. For example, William D. Broderick, director of international governmental research and analysis for Ford Motor Company, asserts that during 1981–82 the car manufacturer managed to trim $300 from the cost of a Ford Escort. But that savings was more than offset, during the same period, by a $900 reduction of the price of an average Japanese car in the United States, thanks to strengthening of the U.S. dollar against the Japanese yen.[24] In the summer of 1983, conservative economist Michael Evans indicated that "a recent study by Evans Economics indicates that if the dollar were devalued by 15–20%, the U.S. economy would return to a competitive position in all major industries except autos and steel."[25] Conversely, the longer the dollar remains overvalued, according to Fred Bergsten of the Institute for International Economics, the more the American economy will encounter trouble. Export-based industry will shrivel, and protectionism may surge. "Throughout the postwar period, dollar over-valuation has been a key 'leading indicator' of an outbreak of protectionist trade pressures."[26]

Moreover, if the crippling role of the overvalued dollar has to be taken as a major caveat against any structural explanation of our troubles, so does another closely linked reality—namely, the excessively high interest rates and expense of capital in the United States. Raising money costs too much here.

A study made for the American Business Conference found that the steep cost of capital in the United States is a major factor in the competitiveness crisis. According to the ABC project director, Thermo Electron Corporation Chairman George Hatsopoulos, a product in 1981 containing $10,000 worth of labor and capital in this country would have cost only $4,900 in Japan. Of the $5,100 differential, $2,800 came from lower wages in Japan, but the other $2,300 came from lower capital costs reflecting Japan's elaborate financial subsidies targeted on favored industries and the Japanese government's practice of suppressing interest rates. In Hatsopoulos's words, "Today, U.S. business faces an almost insurmountable barrier—a cost of capital nearly three times that of their Japanese competitors. The much lower cost of capital services in Japan is consistent with a rate of gross capital formation as a fraction of the Gross National Product, which for Japan is more than double that found in the U.S."[27]

Even the most ardent industrial policy advocate, it would seem to me, has to recognize the potency of several of these macroeconomic arguments, and the case for structural interventionism is thereby undercut.

Vectoring the forces at work, our policy makers must arrive at a synthesis—a meshing of careful nationalism, business-government partnership and chastened macroeconomic awareness—in order to create a workable competitiveness agenda. In the meantime, the crisis of the U.S. economy is already emerging as a major strategic umbrella under which business can marshal support for long-sought tax, export and antitrust objectives. Which suggests a paradox. The political vulnerability of business—its "managerial incompetence"— as identified by Louis Harris in 1981 seems to have eased and perhaps even dissipated, as the left faces the possibility that business can co-opt the industrial strategy issue.* This is so because the complex international dimension of our economic problems has become evident in a way little contemplated by conservative free-market and supply-side advocates in 1980–81 or by industrial policy advocates in late 1982. Increasing tension in global economic circumstances is what requires a cure beyond the reach of conventional political and economic thinking. The challenge is enormous.

*See, for example, *Beyond the Wasteland: A Democratic Alternative to Economic Decline*, by Samuel Bowles, David Gordon and Thomas E. Weisskopf (New York: Anchor Press/Doubleday, 1983). They see conservative economics turning into a contest between monetarism and "the newer entrant in the pro-business policy sweepstakes—which advocates selective government intervention in support of corporate interest and profits." And they suggest that "the corporatists have a better shot at recovery than either the supply-siders or the monetarists."

CHAPTER 2

The Global Economy as a Combat Zone

Some Americans like to believe that a second New Deal—a latter-day Reconstruction Finance Corporation or National Recovery Authority—can restore our competitive economic muscle. But the simple fact is that even the domestic market is slipping beyond our national control—25 percent of the manufactures we consume are imports, up from under 10 percent a decade ago. Major chunks of our own market, from automobile demand in California to electronics sales in New York, are slipping into the hands of foreign neomercantilism as global consumption patterns—the affluent segments in particular—produce global combat zones.

The commercial order of the period before the 1970s—which in broad terms linked Anglo-American supremacy in the financial and industrial West with subservient natural resources economies elsewhere—is breaking down, taking its legal and trading relationships along. The challenge to future American economic well-being lies in simultaneously becoming more assertive of our national self-interest while also trying to promote a new world-wide set of commercial guidelines. The political peril, in the meantime, is that, in their frustration and bewilderment, opinion leaders and the public will try to recover an unrecoverable past.

Yet because global interdependence is a reality, not just a trite phrase, it doesn't seem likely we can retreat into economic isolationism—by attempting to return to the days when tariffs safeguarded our industries and markets as effectively as the Atlantic and Pacific oceans safeguarded our security. Other less obvious backward-looking political economics are also being offered, be they the supply-side dream to re-create the economics of F. Scott Fitzgerald's ballyhoo era, old-line liberal attempts to recapture the New Deal glory days of the Blue Eagle, or foreign-policy establishment reveries about the postwar era of U.S. and Western European hegemony and free-trade leadership. None of these comprehends the new political economics.

Admittedly, no one knows how long the new economic nationalism—"neomercantilism" is another term used to describe the phenomenon—will last and how intense it will become. What's going on here, however, runs deeper than the current workings of the business cycle, and it's to this larger reality that U.S. trade and industrial strategy must respond.

To begin with, one can suggest that the apparent trend toward adoption of an industrial policy among existing and aspiring economic powers is a reaction to global upheaval, and that present-day mercantilist efforts are attempts to cope with international economic realignment. All around the world, the geography of manufacturing is shifting, and countries that do not practice economic self-aggrandizement of a sort—industrial policy being one variant—may come through the global transition economically diminished. On the other hand, the tensions and disruptions of the new economic rivalry are already pointing to the very clear need for a new international collaboration: an agreement about what rules must govern the new techniques of trade and industrial nationalism.

American politicians have certainly responded to the decline in our global competitiveness. In April 1983, officials of the National Academy of Sciences went to Capitol Hill to discuss its report that deplored the growth of trade restraints and industrial policies overseas and called for U.S. strategy in response. A few years earlier, the analysis of the group might have seemed bold; this time, it provoked dismissal. Senator Lloyd Bentsen of Texas observed: "I think it's time to discard the shopworn conventional wisdom and free-trade rhetoric. It's time to start using our market leverage and to negotiate in America's enlightened self-interest. This country is still fighting by Marquess of Queensberry rules against an international trading community of black-belt karate experts."[1]

A few weeks later, former Secretary of State Henry Kissinger, one of America's more notable practitioners of realpolitik, told a Wharton School of Finance symposium on "Removing Obstacles to Economic Growth" that too many economists and business leaders are ignoring harsh diplomatic and political realities. Wise persons, he said, had better start thinking about how to live in a world without free trade because no one is doing anything serious at the international level to alter the prevailing trend toward increased protectionism and old-fashioned mercantilism.[2]

At roughly the same time, Lionel Olmer, Undersecretary of Commerce for International Trade, told executives in Dallas, "What we have developing internationally is a kind of neo-mercantilism to promote exports. . . . If allowed to continue that would be disastrous because there would be no winners."[3]

That's the solitary, nasty and brutish world of Thomas Hobbes they're describing. Hobbes, it might be recalled, was the seventeenth-century English political philosopher whose writings, notably *Leviathan* (1651), make the observation that mankind's state of nature was greedy and bloodthirsty. By corollary, in the arena of international relations, Hobbes said, individual nations live as so many individual people. By this he meant that they "are in continual jealousies and in the state and posture of gladiators; having their weapons pointing, and their eyes fixed, on one another; that is, their forts, garrisons and guns upon the frontiers of their kingdoms, and continual spies upon their neighbors; which is a posture of war. But because they uphold thereby the industry of their subjects, there does not follow from it that misery which accompanies the liberty [license] of particular men."[4] Substitute "trade ministries, national industrial policies and export subsidies" for "forts, garrisons and guns" and you have neomercantilism of the 1980s. Ironically, the original mercantilism—and a very Hobbesian policy it was—flowered in Hobbes's own century, across the Channel under French Finance Minister Jean-Baptiste Colbert.

This is not meant to be a quaint, scholarly digression. A late 1983 Louis Harris international poll, with data from nine countries, shows the strength of neomercantilism in the latter-day West (see table 4). The recurrence of economic nationalism and beggar-thy-neighbor attitudes abroad in the world today suggests that there's little prospect in the 1980s to return to *status quo ante* of the free global marketplace. Accordingly, the choice for us appears to be between an assertive but calculated national trade and industrial strategy, designed to support pressure for new global rules, and a dangerous world-wide escalation of outright protectionism and neomercantilism. It is also tempting to suggest that much of the disarray of the old

TABLE 4.
Protectionist Sentiment in the United States,
Europe and Japan, 1983

	Favor Import Restrictions (%)	Oppose Import Restrictions (%)
United States	63	31
Great Britain	53	36
Italy	53	21
France	48	40
Norway	45	47
Spain	43	31
Germany	39	27
Japan	35	33
The Netherlands	29	47

SOURCES: Based on a poll by the Atlantic Institute for International Affairs/
Louis Harris—France, Philadelphia *Inquirer,* November 29, 1983 (with additional unpublished data furnished by the *Inquirer*).

political economics—especially notions of free markets and free trade
—can be explained by rereading Hobbes on tribalism. If so, that undercuts the new, trendy view that decentralization of global economic
loyalties is a happy, optimistic, creative new reality. What, then,
is the narrowing of perceived economic self-interest around the world
—Hobbesian tribalism or Third Wave self-fulfillment? The way
we answer that question bears heavily on what kind of global economic policy must be shaped to comport with the realities of the 1980s.

COMPETING VIEWS OF THE WORLD ECONOMY

Taken historically, the views of the so-called Atari Democrats and
futurists—two camps favoring a bold embrace of a high-tech economy—seem unrealistic within a common dimension: namely, their
view of what makes human beings and societies tick. There is quite
a distance from Hobbes and Henry Kissinger to Alvin Toffler,
prophet of so-called Third Wave industries, who argues that markets
are "demassifying" and breaking up into small, continuously changing sectors. Production, too, is demassifying, especially in some high-
tech areas. He says that "even if it means a powerful fight against
Second Wave [older manufacturing] industries and trade unions, we

need to put our primary emphasis on developing the Third Wave Sector."[5] Alas, that's much too simple a thesis.

The Benign Demassification Thesis

For Toffler, the Third Wave future pivots on electronics, communications and lasers, as well as on "alternative energy, ocean science and space manufacturing, ecological engineering and eco-system agriculture," all a far cry from the giant factory concentrations of mass manufacturing. And he also suggests that production is regionalizing in a way that involves a "shift from national to smaller than national production. Today, when we look at Kyushu in southern Japan, or Scotland, or Quebec, or Texas, we find regional economies that have become as large and complex as national economies were only a few decades ago."[6]

The trouble is, futurists assume too benign an economic and political environment. "Small is not only beautiful but bountiful," one might now say. Much the same prognosis emerges from analyst John Naisbitt's recent book *Megatrends*.[7] The transition from a national economy to a world economy and global interdependence is painted with optimistic brushstrokes: "High-Tech High Touch"—the idea of a compensating human behavior shift for every successful technological advance—will conquer all. Meantime, the accompanying diffusion of power in our economy is perceived as constructive. So the general thesis here is that decentralization of power parallels the demassification of industry. The industrial revolution, as taught in schoolbooks, was America's great centralizing force, drawing masses of people to mass-production centers, which we don't need in a new high-tech information economy. Workers can be anywhere. What's more, decentralization—a return to smaller forms of economic, cultural and community organization—is also a return to our "natural condition." Institutions predicated on mere production are crumbling. Labor unions are dinosaurs. And decentralization also enlarges popular choice. Specialized stores are booming as production becomes customized. Television networks are losing audiences to cable vendors. Policy making is also decentralizing. States and municipalities are gaining power. Self-help is booming, as is entrepreneurialism. Worker and employee rights are growing as informal networks replace pyramidal hierarchies.

There is considerable truth in this view, so the optimists among us like to think that the world of 2001 will be a place of decentralized yet affluent living. Unpleasant realities such as trade wars and widening gaps between the haves and have-nots are left out. But for most blue-collar Americans the blessings of the information economy will come slowly, at best. Nor does one read about ghetto black neighborhoods in futurist tracts.

For all their easy talk about the new interdependent global economy, many futurists tend to ignore obvious sources of potential disaster. What is Mexico to do with the hundred million people it will have by the year 2000? Not to speak of China or India. At the moment, these countries, along with Korea, Brazil and others, are putting more people to work in low-wage steel, textile and petrochemical industries, and as a result they are emerging as a major threat to the basic industries of the United States and Western Europe. The workers in the factories of Pennsylvania and the Ruhr who find themselves displaced as a result will not necessarily have an enjoyable post-industrial future.

All in all, the general notion that a decentralized, demassified America faces a bright high-tech, Third Wave global future seems overstated, given growing neomercantilism and economic nationalism. The truth is that our economy and social order cannot simply yield steel, textiles and petrochemicals to the Third World while we skip off to high-tech nirvana. Third Wave proponents don't see any need for a trade and industrial strategy, in part because they ignore global economic nationalism and assume high-tech trends play out favorably. This is not a prudent way to look at matters.

A Theory of Economic Balkanization

My own explanation of the centralization, fragmentation and parochialization of outlooks was first published in 1978 in an essay, "The Balkanization of America."* Small is sometimes beautiful or bountiful, but often enough small is parochial. In the the West, loyalties, commitments and identifications over the last ten to fifteen years have been narrowing on virtually every dimension. Nationalism, regionalism, sectionalism and ethnicity are intensifying, as are biological subcategorical identifications—black, female, gay. National, regional and group economic rivalries have also heated up. If futurists have happily linked economic decentralization to the decline of

*Harper's Magazine, May 1978.

mass industry, an analysis more fully grounded in a reading of history can conjoin those splintering loyalties in part at least to the imperial decline of the West. In no small measure, the various parochialisms and turnings inward of Western nations have grown as the glories of being British, French or American have ebbed—not just as the factories have closed, but as the flags of empire have also been hauled down. In short, decentralization and parochialization create problems as well as opportunities.

If the marketplace is Balkanizing both domestically and globally, a new government role—and a new challenge—come into play. In this regard, it's important to consider evidence of the extent to which economic Balkanization is omnipresent: international, national, regional, municipal, group and even ethnic. Consider the dynamics on each of the following dimensions:

- Multinational groupings are emerging as obstacles to free trade and free dissemination of data. Third World nations are pushing for new copyright rules that would allow undeveloped nations to take over rights, for Third World prohibition of the sale of certain products, and the like.
- The behavior of individual nations needs no amplification. Besides embracing neomercantilist industrial policies, many are raising various forms of trade barriers and nontariff restraints on the flow of goods, services and even data.
- Within nations, there is growing evidence that states and regions are turning protective. A number of U.S. states are beginning to require that public employee pension fund monies be partially invested in enterprises within the state in question. Some are developing a state "buy locally" policy. Many other states are debating legislation to block coporations from shutting down businesses (over a certain size) within their borders. Increasingly popular state severance taxes, in turn, are essentially export taxes. The Great Lakes states have discussed Common Market arrangements, and a similar Dixie Common Market possibility has been raised by Florida Governor Robert Graham.
- On an ever-smaller geographic scale, cities are taking advantage of a recent U.S. Supreme Court decision allowing them to favor municipal citizens in employment, contracts and similar matters.
- Finally, it's also clear that economic Balkanization is increasing on a group basis. Black Americans—via Jesse Jackson's PUSH organization—are seeking (and making) deals with major corporations

based on the theory that if blacks constitute 15 percent of a company's market, then 15 percent of its expenditures should be made in the black community via employment, contracts, franchises, bank deposits and the like. Hispanics are weighing their own version of PUSH. Labor unions, meanwhile, are mobilizing their massive pension fund clout to try to keep corporations from moving from the Rust Bowl to the Sun Belt and for other purposes.

Neomercantilism, then, is part of a larger parochialization. Moreover, if one recalls European history, nationalism has tended to intensify during the major periods of progress in commerce and modes of production, notably during the sixteenth and nineteenth centuries. I don't think that is a coincidence. As one horizon (economic) broadens, a second (political) parochializes. International-competition objectives often require increased government involvement, and as official roles grow, markets that were more or less free tend to become political. And as more and more governments assert parochial interests, other governments become the only effective vehicles of response.

My view of what is happening calls for increasing U.S. government commitment to trade and industrial strategy, while notions of benign demassification comport with laissez-faire or libertarian optimism.

THE END OF THE FREE-TRADE ERA

During the last ten years, the role of government in global trade has increased along three lines: business-government partnerships, countertrade or barter, and negotiation of voluntary export restraints. Many in the United States and Britain now think that the era of free trade is over, with the old free-trade model increasingly irrelevant to policy making. In Britain, the "Cambridge School" of economists has been arguing as much for a number of years. Now a substantial body of opinion in the United States has begun to move in the same direction.

University of Michigan professors Alan V. Deardorff and Robert M. Stern, in a paper prepared for the Aspen Institute in 1983, note that the case for free trade rests on a model of the world in which there is assumed to be perfect competition, an absence of market impediments, ample time for markets to adjust and a technology that changes slowly.[8] Today's realities, they suggest, raise the possibility that such assumptions are so outdated that they vitiate the entire doctrine. In an article for *Foreign Affairs* published in 1983, Robert Reich says a new real-world model for trade—reflecting cartels, state subsidies, rapid diffusion of technology and government activity—is needed and U.S. policy should be revised accordingly. To Reich, "The classic principle of free trade no longer offers any practical or politically compelling alternative to protectionism," and he cites the "recent collapse of free trade ideology into retaliatory protectionism."[9]

In related fashion, economist Robert Heilbroner thinks we are moving into a new era that will see "abandonment of the idea of a unified world market as the global basis for accumulation, and its replacement with a system of regional blocs, each securing a reasonably protected market for its favored products, and regulating its intercourse with other large blocs."[10]

Developments in the United States indisputably demonstrate the erosion of free trade. In a study for the Center for the Study of American Business, former Council of Economic Advisers Chairman Murray Weidenbaum observed, "To put the matter bluntly, our hands—as a nation—are not clean when it comes to championing freer flows of world trade and investment."[11] Our trading partners have been asked to abide by "voluntary" quotas on steel and automobiles. Beef import restrictions also apply from time to time. And American textile and apparel industries are sheltered by both quotas and tariffs. Meanwhile, foreign companies complain that our food and drug regulations work as very effective protectionist measures. In late 1982, U.S. Trade Representative William Brock, in a confidential memo, catalogued the industry-by-industry support for additional protectionism (see chapter 3). During 1983, those pressures led to new U.S. quotas and tariffs even before the election year put pressure on Congress.

Currently, our free-trade posture consists more and more of pretense. Even as long ago as 1982, a survey by William Cline of the Institute for International Economics in Washington identified tariff levels as roughly the same among the major nations, while the available measures of nontariff barriers, including mandatory and voluntary quotas, indicated "there can be no automatic presumption that the United States has a substantially more open market than those of its major trading partners."[12] Yet another 1982 survey, this one by Washington's Japan Economic Institute of America, a research organization financed by the Japanese government, had found that at least thirty-six U.S. states limited government purchases of foreign-made products through buy-American legislation, regulation or informal policies. Twenty-four limited the use of foreign steel in highway and bridge construction and other public projects. Seven barred governments from purchasing foreign-made cars or trucks.[13]

On occasion, official U.S. attitudes can be amusing. Charles Maechling of the Carnegie Endowment for International Peace has described one U.S. venture into trade legalism. The success of France's Lacoste sport shirts here provoked so much outcry in the domestic apparel industry that Washington intervened with a change in "classification." No longer was Lacoste's famous alligator a mere trademark; it had become a "decoration," and therefore liable to a trebling of the duty. The alligator emblems are now flown in separately.[14]

The question is, what comes next? Liberals and conservatives alike seem to be dividing into two camps: the internationalists—essentially those who either still believe in the reality of free trade or at least believe that a traditional-style restoration is plausible—and the nationalists, drawn to a policy of increasing toughness on behalf of American interests. Almost by definition, given the once overwhelming dominance of free-trade advocates, the trend toward the nationalist camp seems likely to shape policy.

Some canny Europeans have predicted as much all along. The French, in particular, regard free trade as a form of Anglo-American cultural imperialism. The doctrine was first propounded by two Britons—Adam Smith and David Ricardo—in the late eighteenth and early nineteenth centuries, when Britain, in the vanguard of the industrial revolution, wanted open world markets for Manchester textiles and Sheffield cutlery. By the 1930s, when Britain's declining industrial economy led to sentiment for abandoning free trade, the United States would shortly be ready to take up the banner to open markets for Seattle aircraft and New Jersey pharmaceuticals.

Cynics can observe the comparative chronology of British and American political economics. During the last ten years, the United States has begun to veer away from free-trade advocacy, just at the stage when our share of world manufacturing and trade has diminished to the levels at which Britain earlier began to question and then reject free trade. The pattern shows Great Britain, at its mid-nineteenth-century zenith, boasting half the world's manufacturing production. By 1870, that share had declined to 32 percent; by 1910, to 15 percent. The United States, in turn, had about half of the Free World's GNP in 1946. It now has about 30 percent (and only 20–25 percent of Free World manufacturing). By the end of the century, our GNP percentage will probably be down to 20 percent, our manufacturing percentage down to much less.[15]

In constituency and policy terms, British support for free trade began to erode rapidly in some industrial sectors by the 1890s. By the first decade of the twentieth century, the Conservative party embraced a combination of Empire preference and protectionism, but lost at the polls. Tory politicians swung to protectionism again in the 1920s, and a Conservative-dominated government succeeded in pushing through protectionist legislation in 1932. The United States, at its global manufacturing zenith after World War II, assumed Britain's role as the leading advocate of free trade. But by the late 1960s, support had ebbed substantially in certain industries and among organized labor. Now, as our share of global manufactures plummets, the United States appears to be abandoning yesteryear's trade ideology, perhaps for the reason French analysts state—namely, the end of Anglo-American supremacy. And there is now no comparable economic power to enforce hegemony.

My argument, then, is that the erosion of free trade is historical and systemic, not fundamentally the product of the recession and business cycle of the late 1970s and early 1980s. So if macroeconomic policy is not the principal cause, then better macroeconomic policy can be only a mitigant, not a remedy. Here again, it's worth noting the analysis of Harvard University's Raymond Vernon, a leading scholar of multinational corporate enterprise.

> People carry an image around in their heads about trade policy, and the image usually says that while in periods of prosperity we don't worry too much about competition, in periods of depression we start to put on restrictions. There is nothing in history which suggests that is a correct generalization.
>
> The highest tariffs in the history of the United States were enacted by the Congress, almost absent-mindedly, after eighteen months of not really debate but of horsetrading, following one of the longest periods of prosperity in U.S. history. The debates started in 1928, and the act was passed in the Spring of 1930 as the Hawley-Smoot tariff, at a time when not one person in ten thought we were headed for a deep recession.
>
> The most courageous act of trade liberalization that occurred, oc-

curred at the depths of the Depression, the Trade Agreements of 1934. As you look at the principal (liberalizing) enactments of the Congress since World War Two, they have almost always occurred in troubled times; in 1948, when we were still worrying about the post-war transition; in 1962, when we thought we were in a recession; and in 1974, when we were groggy from the impact of the oil embargo.[16]

Important implications for a policy shift abound if one concludes that the current protectionist mood has not really stemmed from the recession but from a larger upheaval—the winding down of the successive Anglo-American global hegemonies followed by a wave of neomercantilism and trade rival government participation in the marketplace. Professor Vernon observes, "We are talking about moving into an unknown territory on a very broad front, much more important than GATT [General Agreement on Trade and Tariffs], for now the discussion forces us into the whole industrial policy area. So this is the world, distinctly of the third best. My guess is that something like that is what people will push for simply because the other alternatives might not be available."[17]

TRADE AND INDUSTRIAL STRATEGY AS A "MIDDLE WAY"

Rhode Island, Indiana and Texas are full participants in the global Hobbesian mood. The Atlantic Institute poll data cited earlier (see table 4) suggests that the United States may be the most protectionist of major Western economic powers. As table 5 shows, American support for overt protectionist measures—tariffs, import restraints, domestic content laws—reached unprecedented heights in survey data gathered in 1982 and 1983. If academicians are starting to doubt the free-trade model, public doubts have been a lot stronger for a lot longer. Moreover, although protectionist sentiment is especially strong in the Rust Bowl, there are no great regional cleavages, nor are there any great distinctions between the opinions of Democrats and Republicans, conservatives and liberals. What does emerge is an important gap when public opinion about U.S. trade policy is broken down according to income, education and expertise. Blue-collar workers are scared and mad. Better-educated Americans mix more calculation and restraint with their anger. The view here is that to shut down U.S. borders with tariffs and

TABLE 5.
U.S. Public Support for Protectionism

	Favored (%)	Opposed (%)
Tariffs on foreign food products and manufactured goods from countries with high tariffs on U.S. products*	70	22
Limited imports of some goods to protect U.S. jobs even if it results in higher prices*	68	24
Tariffs on Japanese goods to improve balance of trade†	60	31
Restrictions on trade to protect U.S. industry and jobs†	68	26
Increased taxes on foreign goods to protect U.S. jobs in certain industries‡	55	36

*Penn-Schoen (Garth Analysis) Survey, February 1983.
†Los Angeles *Times* poll, May 1983.
‡Gallup/*Newsweek* poll, May 1983.

Note: An Opinion Research Corporation poll, February 1983, indicated that 28% of those polled favored restrictions on all imports, 41% favored restrictions on some imports, and 27% felt that American business should compete without import restrictions.

import restrictions would be self-defeating, and that there must be a better way to fight back.

There is.

A market-oriented competitiveness strategy—though it has yet to take decisive shape in current political discourse—constitutes a middle way between primitive, counterproductive protectionism and free-market acquiescence, between neomercantilism and supineness. One can even say that policy movement in this direction is a critical step if we are to develop a new framework within which global trade is to take place. The Japanese themselves indirectly suggested as much, as they reacted to Houdaille Industries' petition in 1982 that the U.S. government in effect declare Japan's industrial policy an unfair trade practice. Unnamed Japanese officials were quoted observing that their American counterparts could better spend their time thinking about industrial policy in the United States than in Japan. As one senior official told the New York *Times*, "industrial policy is really an American domestic issue—whether you should adopt one or not."[18] In other words, industrial policy—or, in the lesser version I would recommend, a new kind of business-government partnership—is a stage in the evolution of the world economy that the United States, too, must enter. In April 1983, Robert C. Angel, president of the Japan Economic Institute, told an Indianapolis audience that U.S. business should immediately create an information and lobbying organization in Tokyo "to do the grubby things that other countries do in Washington." Angel also suggested that the United States has to spell out a national economic and trade agenda and join the rest of the developed world on the "industrial policy bandwagon."[19]

Far-reaching industrial policy? Probably not. But the idea of an industrial strategy to promote our international economic advantage seems more and more compatible with various public psychologies. The idea that the American mentality is so innocent and open that the public will balk at moving in the new direction appears unfounded. Poll data indicate substantial support for business-labor collaboration, export-targeted subsidies, a new approach to trade law, an upgraded federal trade agency and other competitiveness strategy ingredients—points to be examined in chapters 3 and 4. A survey taken in 1981 of middle- and upper-middle-class households in Belgium, England, Holland, France, Italy, West Germany and the United States turned up results that Donald Kanter, chairman of Boston University's department of marketing, characterized as "the Europeanizing of America." Although Americans on the whole remained a bit more optimistic than Europeans, "The concept of the blunt, open-faced American, a guileless Candide-like character, is not a valued stance in the 1980s. In the current environment, this does not help survival as much as hustling and hipsterism—don't trust anybody's motives, maintain a façade and street smarts, historically the European peasant's protection."[20]

For various political, economic and cultural reasons, a growing number of Americans feel that the nation must have some cohesive approach to trade and industrial policy—that it must, in short, display global economic street smarts. New forms of foreign enterprise, of course, are the decisive spur to action. LICIT, calling the overseas growth of national industrial policies "only the beginning stages of a form of competition for international markets which is based on a cooperative effort of national governments and their industries," argues that "an activist U.S. approach is required to meet the challenge."[21]

Meanwhile, Raymond Vernon is afraid that because we are headed for a world in which many of the trade deals, large and small, are done by governments, there is the possibility that the United States will be too slow to adjust. "The whole American philosophy," he says, "about holding down the transactional role of government is so deep-seated, and the division of governmental powers in America so diffuse, that it is possible you cannot have a selective intervention in the United States: every time you try it, everyone will also want a piece of the pie." Vernon suggests that if the United States does not move toward activism, "There is a risk in this international system [that] the United States will be the dodo-bird, the dinosaur, the non-adapter."[22]

Management expert Peter Drucker argues that there is no alternative but to build an awareness and a concern for trade and comparative economic strength into government policy making. In a 1983 article written for the *Wall Street Journal*, he set out three approaches: (1) an "internationalist" model, which would simply make sure that the economic and foreign-trade consequences of proposed government policies are weighed, but without any aggrandizing ideology; (2) a "nationalist" model, which would examine policy decisions with a commitment to strengthen our economic position in the world market; and (3) a "mercantilist" model, in which bolstering the nation's competitive position in the world market is the principal objective. Drucker favors the internationalist model as the one to best fit American political traditions, but he acknowledges that existing national patterns are usually mixed.[23]

My own feeling is that the domestic political mobilization required to move government policy from passive to active requires adopting what Drucker describes as the nationalist model. Government will have to display a more aggressive commitment to strengthening our economic position in the world market. By and large, however, this will be more a question of trying to open up foreign markets that are now not free than of protecting our own markets.

Business leaders, too, have found themselves groping to define the irony that a new national assertiveness may be the key to an effective new internationalism. Du Pont Chairman Edward Jefferson, in urging a "pro-industrial strategy," has called for pressing other countries to open their markets to our companies by using "our own

lucrative domestic market as leverage."[24] In regard to policy, his
position is a hybrid—elements of protectionism, but with a free-trade
goal. In a late 1983 speech to the Cleveland Rotary Club, Richard
P. Simmons, president of Allegheny Ludlum Corporation, said:
"You may describe me as a 'free trade–protectionist,' committed
to the same protection under U.S. law that I would have from any
domestic competitor who attempted to drive me out of business
illegally. . . . I believe that protectionism which protects against
illegal, subsidized trade does not contravene the concepts of free
trade."[25] And these men are hardly alone. Scores of their colleagues
find themselves giving speeches calling for the government in Washington to enter the new world economic struggle with policies that
join assertion of American overseas ambitions with more effective
control of foreign access to the huge American market—and all in
the name of a new internationalism.

The paradox is not easily set straight, but I think they are correct.
Only a policy aimed at strengthening our global competitiveness—
Peter Drucker's "nationalist" yardstick—is likely to be taken seriously enough in the world community to enable Washington to make
the case for building a new set of trade "fences" to help make the
major Western nations better economic neighbors. So taken, a hard-
boiled competitiveness strategy may actually be a prerequisite to
setting the scene for a new internationalist trading order. It's my
feeling that it is now possible to lay down the basis for a set of ideas
and a supporting political agenda to make the United States the
prime mover for progress.

CHAPTER
3

Industries, Business Organizations and Citizens: Support for a New Competitiveness Agenda

Restoring our national economic competitiveness has become a major political concern. Issue after issue—jobs, quality education, high tech, the value of the dollar, the soaring trade deficit—has developed within and fueled the larger debate. Notwithstanding the frustrations of the country's changing role in world markets, a constituency can be marshaled for a constructive agenda—for an agenda that channels public frustration and government action into assertive rather than protective form.

Businessmen are now taking the lead in invoking government power and assistance. Du Pont Chairman Edward Jefferson has called for "an effective pro-industrial strategy . . . a process in which industrial and government policies are developed not just to respond to changing world markets, but to anticipate them."[1] John C. Marous, president of Westinghouse International, put it a bit differently:

> We shouldn't invest the idea of [liberal] industrial policy with too many dreams of magic. Our government already has the power to help industry in a variety of ways.
>
> It can stop hindering the operations of trade. Many of the greatest impediments to American business efforts overseas come from a lack of clarity in the legal ground rules. Myriad constraints—in our Foreign Corrupt Practices Act or the antitrust laws, for example—present a legal labyrinth for international-minded companies. Moreover, such difficul-

ties as those laws present are self-imposed—on Americans, by Americans. Government alone has the power to remove them.

Government can put the State Department to work in support of American companies overseas. It can help businesses get more competitive export financing. It can promote research and development by making it easier for companies to set up joint ventures and by encouraging reinvestment of earnings.

Government can help to level the playing field where foreign competitors have been helped by their own governments. It does not have to resort to protectionism; it can use its weight to assure that competing nations play by the same rules.[2]

This broader invocation of government assistance and authority is all too often misunderstood. What is developing is not by any means protectionism. But as Professor Chalmers Johnson told the National Association of Manufacturers task force on foreign industrial policies in October 1983, "I would suggest that there could be no more devastating weakness for any major nation in the 1980s than the inability to define the role of government in the economy."[3]

Precisely. And the list of aggrieved and concerned companies, industries, trade associations and labor unions is by no means as restricted—in either geographical or ideological terms—as some critics imply. Almost as many Sun Belt corporations can be found on the list as Frost Belt firms, and very few are proposing old-style "protectionism." It's very hard to overstate the interest of corporate executives and business organizations. Scarcely a major group has stayed out of the competitiveness debate, and the recommendations are notable not only for content but for volume and frequency. These activities may go a long way to co-opt the industrial policy debate and give it what du Pont Chairman Jefferson terms a "pro-industrial" coloration.

One can also say that major parts of the agenda already discussed by various business groups conform to the general shape of public opinion. The man in the street is as eager for action as the person in the executive suite.

INDUSTRY AND EXECUTIVE ATTITUDES TOWARD TRADE

It helps to look at business opinion from three different perspectives —the new political geography of industry attitudes, industry-by-industry points of view, and a general summary of executive attitudes. The bottom line is that the call for "fair trade" and a "level international playing field" is substantial and growing.

The New Political Geography of U.S. Trade Outlooks

Contrary to public perceptions that companies perturbed about foreign competition are confined to Great Lakes smokestack country, Sun Belt industries also, some of them very young and high-tech, are in the forefront of the demand that Washington develop an assertive international economic strategy. A fast Cook's tour can begin in California. Few industries are louder in calling for action than the semiconductor industries of Silicon Valley around San Jose. The action agenda of the Semiconductor Industry Association based in Cupertino is summarized later. Meanwhile, Charles Sporck of the National Semiconductor Corporation, a blunt chief executive, complains, "We have no plan, no policy for staying competitive in high-tech fields, and until we do, we are in danger of being wiped out industrially by Japan."[4] National Semiconductor is based in Santa Clara.

In Arizona, one of the state's leading employers, the electronics giant Motorola, is a well-known advocate of a hard-line approach to Japan. Texas, too, has a number of industries advocating economic nationalism. LTV Corporation, the giant Dallas-based aerospace conglomerate, sponsored newspaper advertisements in mid-1983 that called free trade an illusion and acknowledged that a national industrial policy might be necessary. And local economists point to the extent to which the Texas Gulf Coast, in particular, relies on declining industries. The dependence includes not just petrochemicals, but also oil refining, steel and shipbuilding. The Texas U.S. House delegation provided strong support for 1983's proposed steel import quota legislation. Next door, in Louisiana, there is also a large concentration of the endangered petrochemical industry, a recognized target of foreign business-government partnerships. Chemical giants like du Pont, Monsanto, Union Carbide and W. R. Grace, among others, are active in trade coalitions like LICIT and CITE.

At the eastern end of the Sun Belt, Florida's high-tech operations include several companies quite visibly calling for a tough trade strategy. Harris Corporation (data processing) is a member of CITE, while Houdaille Industries, in Fort Lauderdale, maker of computerized machine tools, has been the most belligerent firm in the industry. In the Southeast, steel manufacturing in Birmingham, Alabama, the "Pittsburgh of the South," is in serious trouble. Georgia, the Carolinas and Virginia are centers of the beleaguered domestic textile industry. In sum, industries found in the Sun Belt constitute a strong voice for an aggressive economic and trade strategy, as do many Sun Belt labor unions.

Trade frustration is now national, not sectional. Concern about the unfair competition posed by foreign business-government collaboration has spread from troubled basic industries, concentrated in the North and a few older parts of the South, to businesses in the computer, semiconductor, machine tool, optoelectronics and telecommunications sectors. Geographically, the issue is a national one, with economic and population growth areas just as concerned as are the centers of declining industry.

Industry-by-Industry Points of View

There's even an official catalog of national economic frustration. In late 1982 William E. Brock, the U.S. Trade Representative, went so far as to lay out the trade politics in the United States on an industry-by-industry basis. In a confidential memorandum obtained by the Chicago *Tribune,* Brock observed:

> Most U.S. industries and their workers feel that they are competing against not only aggressive foreign firms but also foreign governments while their own government sits on the sidelines. . . . To a considerable extent, this dissatisfaction stems from a belief that the U.S. government does not support our exporters and will not adequately protect U.S. producers against unfair foreign trade practices, either in the United States or third-country markets. . . . The political coalition that has supported an open U.S. trade policy has eroded as the result of our inability to solve key trade issues. Many of the major U.S. industries that have supported an open U.S. trade policy in the past have become disaffected.[5]

Turning to individual industries and setting aside the obvious situations of steel, autos and textiles, Brock had the following observations to make:*

*In January 1984, Brock saw no need to revise his analysis, saying that any changes were only a matter of degree.

Construction equipment: The industry has been "strongly pro–free trade but is undoubtedly rethinking its posture at this time." Executives blame export controls, lack of export financing and an overvalued dollar for their competitive disadvantage with Komatsu, the giant Japanese firm that has made "significant strides in achieving its objective of world market dominance."

Chemicals: "The chemical industry's support of free trade has long been muted because of its recognition that over coming years it will be at a competitive disadvantage vis-à-vis the OPEC countries."

Forest products: The industry is pro–free trade but "chafes under European and Japanese protectionism."

Aircraft: While the industry is "still free trade, concern is deep." Airbus, the European consortium, has recently outsold Boeing and McDonnell-Douglas because of its multigovernment support and assistance. "In contrast, the industry feels the U.S. government hinders their efforts internationally through export controls, the Foreign Corrupt Practices Act and lack of political-level support. Further, because of our antitrust statutes, the industry is entering into joint venture arrangements with our competitors, but is not able to collaborate among themselves. Finally, the industry is concerned with the availability of export credits."

High tech: The industry is especially worried about the Japanese threat and the "history of U.S. government neglect." Independent semiconductor producers "appear to be moving protectionist and support for free trade but other high-tech portions of the [electronics] industry is declining."

Machine tools: The industry "is extremely worried about high Japanese import penetration of the U.S. market, which it feels is supported by a government-sponsored cartel. . . . The industry is poised to press for import relief, alleging that it should be protected on national security grounds."

Agriculture: Long a bastion of free-trade sentiment, not least because exports accounted for 20 percent of farm income, "it too is becoming disenchanted with this administration's ability to deal with foreign unfair trade practices, such as subsidies."

By this estimate, it's obvious that the traditional free-trade alignments are no longer in place. For a century or so, from the 1820s to the 1930s, the manufacturing sections of the country—New England initially, but eventually pretty much the entire industrial North—

favored a protective tariff. They got it, and prospered. During that period the principal free-trade advocacy was based in the agricultural South and West. Then later, in our economic heyday after World War II, free-trade support issued from all over the country. The only dissenting voices were those of a few declining industrial areas, especially parts of New England and the Southern textile centers. On the face of it, at least, today's changing alignment suggests a reversion. By the 1970s, protectionist sentiment was growing in the Great Lakes heavy industries, like steel and autos, and by the early 1980s frustration about trade had spread to major portions of the high-tech sector and agriculture. As of now, there is no longer a geographically definable majority coalition for unrestricted free trade in the United States.

In his 1982 memorandum, Brock acknowledged that trade-related problems would not end with a business cyclical upturn. Which is certainly true. We are at a trade policy watershed in which the ideology of the Truman, Eisenhower, Kennedy and Johnson years no longer commands public adherence. Instead, we are seeing the slow and tentative replacement of the ideological, regional and interest-group coalition for free trade with a new national coalition for fair or reciprocal trade. Do unto us as you would have us do unto you, one could say. Yet because the new grouping stops far short of protectionism in the old sense, while at the same time it is very unhappy about foreign mercantilism's new techniques, it seems appropriate to call the new coalition more assertive than protective.

Executive Support for Fair Trade, Not Protectionism

The terms used can be important, and in this instance, they are. As he set out the changing trade views of leading U.S. industries, Brock routinely characterized their dissatisfaction as "protectionism." That's not only unnecessarily pejorative, but also misleading. First, the new international trading realities go a long way to justify unhappiness with lingering U.S. free-trade pretenses. Second, polls suggest that small businessmen tend toward protectionism, while executives of major corporations by and large do not. To be sure, the latter believe Japanese trading practices are unfair—by 72 to 19 percent, according to a 1982 *Business Week*/Louis Harris poll.[6] But who doesn't? And 85–90 percent favor a shift of U.S. policy toward a system of reciprocity, according to Harris's and other surveys. There is little support in Fortune 500 corporate suites for overt protectionism, however—increased tariffs, broad usage of import quotas or domestic content legislation. As a matter of fact, Harris's survey found 66-percent opposition to increased tariffs. A 1982 U.S. Chamber of Commerce poll found that major corporation executives opposed domestic content legislation by 56 percent to 25 percent.[7]

In December 1982, a Gallup/*Wall Street Journal* poll found only 23 percent of executives of major corporations supporting import restraints.[8] Free trade has broken down, yes; but among executives of large companies, at least, majority support for fair trade, not protectionism, has taken its place.

Most businessmen would prefer an affirmative agenda. Tables 6 and 7 show recent survey data on corporate executive support for specific competitiveness remedies, including the general notion of reciprocity. Bankers and service industry executives are also moving toward fair trade and reciprocity. Enough industries are involved—and a substantial-enough weight of executive opinion—to add up to a mandate for action.

But beyond generalized industry viewpoints and the collective opinion of executives as evidenced by surveys, we must also look at the wide range of proposals drawn up by various business organizations, ad hoc coalitions and task forces. These are the vehicles through which corporate America has made major contributions toward creating a competitiveness agenda.

BUSINESS ORGANIZATIONS AND THE U.S. ECONOMIC COMPETITIVENESS AGENDA

How times have changed. Fifty years ago, businessmen scoffed at the "alphabet agencies" set up in Washington to try to fight the Great Depression—the CCC, WPA, NRA, TVA and so forth. Now corporate America's own array of alphabet organizations has been a prime source of proposals for reasserting U.S. economic interests. So much so, in fact, that by noting the recurrent ideas and suggestions, it's possible to discern the outline of a business consensus. Or at least a strategic center of gravity. And when that outline is matched with public opinion and the collective clout of interest groups and constituencies, the rough shape of what could be a national competitiveness coalition takes form.

No one looking for a handle on a program for the major economic remobilization coming from the business community can get very far

TABLE 6.
*Business Executives' Opinions on Proposals to
Spur U.S. Trade Competitiveness*

	Opinion Research Corp., 1983 (%)	Harris/ Business Week, 1982–83 (%)	Kane, Parsons, Inc., 1982* (%)
Negotiate with Japan for a stable exchange rate between the dollar and the yen	89	—	—
Pressure foreign governments to open their markets to imports	88	—	—
Strengthen GATT to settle disputes	85	—	—
Increase incentives to retrain workers	76	—	—
Allow private joint-venture research	73	—	—
Increase the funding of the Export-Import Bank	70	—	—
Adopt trade reciprocity posture	—	90	85
Provide greater incentives to American industry to export to Japan, or eliminate disincentives to export	—	—	81
Revitalize U.S. industries through domestic economic or tax policies to achieve higher productivity and make our products internationally competitive	—	—	92
Amend Foreign Corrupt Practices Act to allow payments to foreign officials to speed up or unblock routine government actions	—	65	—

*Taken for Japanese Automobile Manufacturers Association.

without knowing some key names and acronyms: the Aerospace Industries Association, the American Business Conference (ABC), the Business Council, the Business–Higher Education Forum, the U.S. Chamber of Commerce, the Coalition for Employment through Exports, the Coalition of Service Industries (CSI), the Committee for Economic Development (CED), the Committee for International Trade Equity (CITE), the Conference Board, the Emergency Com-

TABLE 7.

Service Industry Chief Executives' Opinions on Proposals to Spur U.S. Trade in Services

	Would Have Slight or Significant Positive Effect (%)	Would Have No Effect (%)	Would Be Counterproductive (%)
Negotiation of bilateral agreements on services with trading partners	87	5	8
Amendment of Foreign Corrupt Practices Act to clarify accounting and antibribery provisions	74	21	5
Creation of a multilateral framework for trade in services under GATT	72	25	3
Creation of a Cabinet-level Department of Trade as proposed by the administration	71	24	8
Simplification of export licensing requirement	68	32	0
Reciprocity legislation requiring U.S. regulators to take into account a foreign country's treatment of U.S. service suppliers in licensing or regulating businesses from that country	65	15	20
Utilization of subsidies and incentives to encourage services exports	61	24	15
Legislation to sharpen application of existing U.S. trade remedies (i.e., Section 301 of 1974 Trade Act) to services	59	29	12
Authorization for President to establish terms and conditions under which foreign service firms may engage in interstate commerce in the United States upon a determination that a foreign country discriminates against U.S. service companies	56	25	18
Preservation and strengthening of DISC regardless of GATT objections	52	31	17
Modification of DISC to meet GATT objections	40	55	5
Local content legislation or services trade restrictions with similar intent	16	36	48
Use of trade as a foreign policy mechanism (sanctions, grain embargo, etc.)	10	22	68

SOURCE: Survey of major service-industry CEOs published in *Business Views on International Trade in Services*, by Price, Waterhouse (1983).

mittee for American Trade (ECAT), the Labor-Industry Coalition
for International Trade (LICIT), the Massachusetts High Technology Council, the National Association of Manufacturers (NAM), the
National Research Council, the New England Council and the Semiconductor Industry Association (SIA). Taken together, their membership includes a majority of America's large corporations, which
should dispel the notion that only a small periphery of American
business supports a substantial activist agenda.*

A caveat is in order here. Many of the companies and industries
involved are concerned about only one or two issues. Firms preoc-
cupied with productivity and capital formation may not see immediate full enforcement of existing U.S. trade laws as a matter of
competitive life and death. So the vague outlines of a possible consensus don't mean that consensus already exists.

To begin with the "nationalist" component: many industries see
existing trade policy and trade law as the preeminent issue. The
Labor-Industry Coalition for International Trade, the Committee
for International Trade Equity and the Semiconductor Industry Association are all up in arms over the impact of foreign industrial
policies on U.S. trade and on major U.S. industries. Ditto for the
major computer and machine-tool trade associations. The principal
focal point of their fear and concern is the targeting by foreign
governments of key industries for maximum assistance.

LICIT issued the most comprehensive report of early 1983 under
the title *International Trade, Industrial Policies and the Future of
American Industry*. Its four major policy recommendations can be
summarized as follows:

1. Existing U.S. trade laws must be enforced and implemented in
a timely and effective manner—which is often not the case today—
and must be updated to give U.S. officials a better weapon to deal
with the unfair trade impact of foreign industrial policies.

2. The U.S. government should move toward a wide variety of
partial "industrial policy" measures—research and development, antitrust modifications, conversion/restructuring assistance, tax code
revision and education/retraining—to strengthen the international

---

*I have skipped over the positions of the American Iron and Steel Institute, the
American Textile Manufacturers Institute and the Motor Vehicle Manufacturers
Association because observers (somewhat unfairly) take their competitiveness views
and concerns as a given.

competitiveness of U.S. industries while avoiding a process of picking winners and losers.

3. The U.S. government must establish a research and information-gathering capacity to evaluate foreign industrial policies and their potential impact on U.S. industries, trade and unemployment.

4. To encourage other countries in the future to limit the effects of their industrial policies on other nations, the United States should prepare for future international negotiations toward common rules governing the use of industrial policy measures that distort international trade and investment.[9]

Much the same agenda comes from the Committee for International Trade Equity (CITE), a group of twenty-one largely high-tech or electronics firms, ranging from Cincinnati Milacron to Control Data and GTE. The committee's January 1983 organizing statement called for working "towards a more effective U.S. public policy with respect to foreign government industrial and targeting policies that distort international free market competition."[10] In this manifesto, the member companies promised to promote three specific goals: first, to create a better domestic environment to promote the international competitiveness of U.S. corporations; second, to prevent market-distorting policies of foreign countries from injuring U.S. corporations; and third, to facilitate international negotiations to eliminate or curb market-distorting foreign practices. In short, to draw a bead on Japanese industrial policy.

Similarly, the California-based Semiconductor Industry Association (SIA) released a detailed study in February 1983 calling for the U.S. government to launch a six-point response to Japan:

1. The U.S. government should announce "that foreign industrial targeting practices will not be allowed to undermine U.S. technological and economic leadership in this critical industrial sector [semiconductors]."

2. The U.S. government "must identify, analyze and counter the distorting effects of foreign industrial targeting practices . . . the U.S. should provide assurances that it will take appropriate action under the U.S. trade laws if monitoring reveals the existence of unfair trade practices."

3. "The U.S. government should insist that U.S. semiconductor

firms receive commercial opportunities in Japan that are fully equivalent to those enjoyed by Japanese firms."

4. "In order to establish the free market competitive conditions
internationally, the U.S. government should promptly seek enforcement of Japan's obligations through consultations and other procedures available under the General Agreement on Tariffs and Trade,
and the subsidies code negotiated in the Tokyo Round of Multilateral Trade Negotiations."

5. "The U.S. government should use the implementation of these
policies with respect to Japan as a model for dealing with targeted
industry practices in other countries."

6. "The U.S. Congress should enact legislation that provides the
authority and means necessary to insure that the U.S. government
can carry out the policies and measures outlined above effectively."[11]

Semiconductor industry executives made a case that while the U.S.
government has remained a passive onlooker, the nation's share of
the semiconductor world export market has dropped from 40 percent
in 1970 to 23 percent in 1980 as the Japanese share has climbed from
6 percent to 25 percent. In April 1983 Clyde Prestowitz, Deputy
Assistant Secretary of Commerce for International Economic Policy,
told a Washington world trade conference that while American
manufacturers produced all of the 1K and 4K memory chips in early
computers, the Japanese captured half of the market for 16K chips
and 70 percent of the market for 64K chips. "The 256K will be all
Japanese," he said.[12] Given these realities, it's not surprising that
American semiconductor and electronics firms are out front in the
fight to convince the government to take strong trade law measures
against foreign industrial policies.

In machine tools, Houdaille Industries helped bring the issue to
a head by filing a petition in 1982 with the U.S. Trade Representative,
saying that purchasers of Japanese machine tools should not qualify
for an investment tax credit, because Japan's economic climate, in
which industries are targeted and assisted by the government,
amounts to a cartel arrangement. Houdaille did not just ask the U.S.
government to find that Japan engages in unfair trade practices; it
also argued that Japan, Inc., is per se an unfair trade practice.

Meanwhile, computer industry spokesmen, talking with Commerce Secretary Malcolm Baldrige in the summer of 1983, took up
essentially the same position. In a joint statement, they called for "a

vigorous program to counter foreign targeting through strict enforcement of U.S. trade laws. . . . Active enforcement would lend integrity to the legal structure now in place." W. J. Sanders, chief executive officer of Advanced Micro Devices, urged: "The U.S. government should announce that foreign industrial targeting practices will not be allowed to undermine U.S. technological and economic leadership." And Data General CEO Edson DeCastro requested adoption of a "no nonsense" policy opposing barriers to free and fair trade, specifically barriers raised by foreign national industrial policies.[13]

In January 1984, the Aerospace Industries Association—representing companies ranging from Honeywell and ITT to big aircraft producers like Boeing, Lockheed and McDonnell-Douglas—published its own blunt call for both a "national trade policy" and a "national industrial research and development policy." And while the AIA rejected an industrial strategy whereby the government would pick winners and losers or would involve itself in economic micromanagement, it simultaneously endorsed policies that "must center on a new commitment and a new philosophy—characterized by a more cooperative relationship between government and industry" in order to compete with foreign business-government partnerships. In the trade policy area, the group specifically rejected protectionism but called for increased export tax incentives, an enlarged capability and aggressiveness for the Export-Import Bank, U.S. government actions to counteract foreign government marketing practices and export subsidies that distort trade, and efforts to promote the further extension of global trade rules. With respect to R&D, the association called for maximum U.S. countermeasures to offset the competitive advantages accruing to foreign manufacturers from the support of their governments, as well as permanent status for the 25 percent R&D tax credit, better treatment of independent research and development (IR&D), encouragement of more effective cooperation among government, industry and the academic community, and modification of the antitrust laws to remove uncertainty regarding collaboration among U.S. firms on research projects.

There's an obvious and substantial coincidence of recommendations among LICIT, CITE and the semiconductor, aerospace, machine tool and computer industries. The point is that indignation over the impact of foreign industrial policies—and over the limited response of the U.S. government—goes beyond the griping of a few companies. Increasingly, it's the strong feeling across a wide spectrum of U.S. industries, ranging from autos, steel and chemicals to electrical generating equipment, data processing and silicon-chip makers. Even a National Academy of Sciences task force and the Business–Higher Education Forum have weighed in with kindred recommendations. More than any other trade issue, the question of foreign industrial policies—and what to do about them—dominated the debate of 1983.

Other coalitions and trade associations are less specific and are simply calling for a new, coordinated American policy, trade law enforcement and assertiveness. Most notably, scores of major and minor business groups have testified before Congress in support of an increased U.S. commitment to trade reciprocity.

To cite one important example, service industries, from banking and insurance to transportation and telecommunications, have long been free-traders but now face growing barriers overseas as foreign countries nurture their own firms. So in testimony taken in June 1983 before the U.S. House Committee on Energy and Commerce, the Emergency Committee for American Trade (ECAT), vehicle of some sixty U.S. multinational corporations, endorsed legislation calling for a new aggressiveness to enumerate and then to try to dismantle foreign obstacles to the export of U.S. services. ECAT observed that "current rules and enforcement procedures are either inadequate or non-existent for trade in agricultural, services and direct foreign investment. In these areas, we must provide our government with authority to negotiate appropriate bilateral and multilateral agreements."[14] And ECAT also backed legislation "calling for compilation of inventories of foreign barriers to U.S. trade in goods, services, and investment, together with a program to alleviate or eliminate such barriers." Service industries have generally favored the U.S. government's December 1983 proposal for adoption by GATT—the General Agreement on Tariffs and Trade—of broad rules for fairness in international trade in services.

In many quarters, there's also a sense that part of our problem is that we don't have an adequate mechanism to frame and pursue a coordinated domestic and international economic strategy. By 1983 key national business organizations like the National Association of Manufacturers, the National Federation of Independent Business, the U.S. Chamber of Commerce and the American Business Conference had lined up to support a critical new institutional requirement

—a new federal Department of International Trade and Industry, to foster trade policy cohesion and coordination. A new Washington lobby—the Coalition for Effective Trade Organization—was created to promote the idea of a unified Cabinet-level operation.

Recognition of the need to improve productivity is also high on the agenda of the new business groups concerned about competitiveness. In May 1983, the Committee for Economic Development (CED), with a largely corporate membership, called for a major business-government effort to reverse the long-term slowdown in the growth of productivity in the U.S. economy. Without such a change, they argued, the United States "faces the very real prospects of reduced standards of living for all its citizens and of a threatened national security."[15] Besides urging removal of impediments to saving and investment by business, the CED urged a change in the labor-management climate—a restructuring of labor-management relationships to create incentives for cooperative action to accept automation and the use of "labor-management participation teams" to give workers a greater say.*

On the fiscal policy front, the American Council for Capital Formation and the American Business Conference have also been active, calling for procapital formation tax law changes. Also, as perceptions of national difficulty broadened in 1983, corporate groups began to issue and urge adoption of increasingly comprehensive agendas. A task force of the Business–Higher Education Forum published a report in May 1983 entitled *America's Competitive Challenge: The Need for a National Response.* In it, sixteen corporate and university presidents called for making restoration of U.S. international competitiveness the "central objective" for the rest of the decade: "Other nations have recognized the new economic imperative and have integrated their domestic foreign policies into aggressive, coordinated national strategies to meet the challenge of international competition. The United States has not. . . . As a nation, we must develop a consensus that industrial competitiveness is crucial to our social and economic well-being."[16]

---

*In April 1984, the CED published a major report opposing the sort of "industrial policy" that would involve an industrial bank or development board able to allocate government assistance to specific industries and companies. What the CED *endorsed* was a "strategy for industrial competitiveness," including tax changes, antitrust reform, trade law revision to deal with unfair international competition, and evolution of a new international legal framework to govern trade in services.

Among the changes recommended are modification of antitrust laws so companies may cooperate in sponsoring basic research; further reductions in the capital gains tax on long-term investments; federal loans for engineering students who agree to become teachers; development of a displaced worker retraining program modeled after the GI bill; appointment of a presidential adviser on economic competitiveness similar to those in fields such as science and national security; and establishment of an information center on international competitiveness in the Commerce Department.

Also in the spring of 1983, the National Task Force on Education for Economic Growth, a group of forty-one educational and corporate leaders and state governors, called for "deep and lasting change" in our educational system to put the country on a par with Japan and other industrial nations. Included were present or former chief executive officers of IBM, Control Data and Texas Instruments.[17]

In the meantime, the chairmen of two major business organizations—Bernard O'Keefe of the National Association of Manufacturers and Arthur Levitt of the American Business Conference—have rejected any form of industrial policy in which the federal government would pick winners and losers. Each recommended, instead, a group of specific competitiveness proposals. In the summer of 1983, O'Keefe urged softening of the antitrust laws, expansion of the Export-Import Bank, amendment of the Foreign Corrupt Practices Act and modification of the Export Administration Act.[18] And Levitt, in the fall of 1983, argued that "an industrial policy for America must reinforce proven patterns of success, and it must include a mandate to target and remove obstacles to real growth in our economy." Among his specific recommendations are tax reform to encourage entrepreneurialism; additional tax incentives for research and development; strict cost-benefit review of environmental, health and safety regulations; and finally, adoption of a "coherent policy of growth [that] must include a demand that our partners in trade dismantle barriers to goods and cease their illegal, unfair subsidies that cheat us out of markets we have earned."[19] In one or two areas, consensus is proving elusive, with nobody saying much. On the issue of retraining, only the Business–Higher Education Forum has called for a major federal program expansion on top of that created by legislation in 1982. Considerably more division prevails in business community ranks here than on most other points.

But the measure of spreading concern in 1983 within the corporate

and university communities can be shown by trying to find a group
that did *not* weigh in with a serious set of recommendations on the
competitiveness issue. Even quasi-official commissions have gotten
into the act. Back in 1982, the National Academy of Sciences assem-
bled a "Panel on Advanced Technology Competition and the Indus-
trialized Allies" composed of fourteen people and headed by Howard
W. Johnson, chairman of the Massachusetts Institute of Technology.
The panel's report, issued in April 1983, spelled out two basic conclu-
sions. First, that the U.S. government must play a larger role in
maintaining the nation's capacity for technological innovation; and
second, that U.S. trade policy must be toughened. The group called
for "the most immediate hard bargaining" against such unfair practices as predatory pricing, the targeting of specific high-tech markets
by foreign governments, restrictions on U.S. direct investment, and
the denying of distribution outlets for our advanced-technology products. Strategically, the panel recommended a set of graduated responses, ranging from bilateral discussions to formal dispute
proceedings. And should all else fail, the United States must take
"unilateral action to protect the national interest."[20]

The recommendations here by no means exhaust statements made
and positions taken by interested business groups, but two basic
points deserve underscoring: first, the extent to which a major element of nationalism—best displayed in trade law militancy and the
desire to pin down foreign predatory practices—is displacing the old
easygoing internationalist point of view; and second, that what these
various blue-ribbon groups have not called for is revealing. Not a
single one has called for a protectionist package of tariffs and quotas.
Nor has any advocated a national industrial development bank or a
latter-day version of the Reconstruction Finance Corporation. And
none have advocated establishing a mechanism to pick "winners and
losers" or to target assistance for presumably promising high-tech
industries. But within a workable, practical, moderate and restrained
set of ideas, most of the country's major business organizations have
offered programs that add up to a basis for a serious national trade
and industrial strategy.

The important thing about the many and various groups calling
for a national economic strategy is not simply the strength and
validity of their suggested remedies, but also the sheer volume of
their policy statements and their insistence that action be taken. The
magnitude of business establishment attention evident here will no

doubt result in a significant response from politicians and policy makers.

PUBLIC SUPPORT FOR A NEW ACTIVIST AGENDA

Measured against executive and business organization opinion, the public mood has been considerably more fierce. If major elements of the corporate community have shown inclination to flirt with trade restraints, the electorate is ready for a serious affair. Nevertheless, despite the extent of public support for traditional protective measures shown in table 5 in the trade war with Japan, there's also widespread support for a new business-labor-government partnership and for a wide range of affirmative measures to promote the global competitiveness of our corporations. Specific-issue public opinion data, where available, are given later, but for a general assessment of public response, it's enough to say that back in 1980 and 1981 the American electorate believed that government regulation had gone too far and that reduction of government constraints would help business get back on its feet. Voters looked askance at the idea of more government involvement. Now public opinion seems to have swung toward Washington's taking a more activist approach.

Given the right national agenda, I think we can discount, or at least rechannel, protectionist sentiments among the public. The sharp contrast between opinion leaders' 80–90-percent opposition to domestic content legislation, import restrictions or increased tariffs and 55–70-percent public support for such measures doesn't inevitably mean conflict—at least, not with effective leadership. A careful observer can also plot a lot of common affirmative ground to link the public and the Fortune 500—support for reciprocal trade policies, endorsement of new trade laws, antitrust and export promotion approaches, backing for increased business-government-labor collaboration, and endorsement of programs to improve our scientific research and development, productivity, product quality, education and worker retraining. In short, the flip side of public apprehension over the decline of our economy is a willingness to be mobilized for a new domestic activism as well as for protective measures against external economic foes.

Popular frustration will, of course, tend to ebb and flow with the business cycle. Yet the extent of public concern seems well established. A national survey taken for the New York Stock Exchange in the spring of 1983 found 65 percent of those queried saying America is still a very important world power, but that "our economic position is seriously declining around the world—and most respondents are angry about this decline."[21] Another national sampling, in May 1983 for the Los Angeles *Times*, likewise found the electorate greatly upset. Support for restrictions on foreign goods was "so strong that many Americans are willing to accept the unfavorable consequences of protectionist policies."[22]

The public also seems responsive to the idea that lackadaisical, uncoordinated policy positions must change. A 1981 survey conducted by Cambridge Reports for Union Carbide found Americans convinced that new conditions in the world required our linking domestic economic policies with trade strategies. Here is the way the question was put, along with the results:[23]

Some people say that the world economy and the U.S. economy are linked so closely together that the U.S. can't solve either its economic problems at home or in the world at large by attacking them separately. These people say that the time has come for the U.S. to shape its economic policies and programs so that they take our problems both at home and abroad into account. Other people say that U.S. economic problems aren't linked that closely to the world economy, and that we don't have to take the world economy into account in shaping our economic policies. Which is closer to your opinion?

The U.S. economy is so closely linked to the world economy that we can't solve our economic problems by attacking them separately	54%
The U.S. economy is *not* so closely linked to the world economy that we have to take the world economy into account in shaping our own economic policies	23%
Don't know	23%

Part of what Americans are looking for is a new spirit of institutional cooperation. Back in 1980, an earlier Cambridge Reports national sampling for Union Carbide had found "almost universal agreement that our difficult economic problems . . . are exacerbated by needless conflicts among the various sectors of society. And the public said they want all of our institutions—including government and business —to work together more closely to solve these problems."[24]

New York Stock Exchange Chairman William Batten found the same mood permeating his organization's 1983 poll results: "They [the American people] are telling us, I believe, that they are fed up with our traditional counterproductive adversary relationships—the purely partisan debates in government, and the ongoing hostility between management and labor, and between labor and business."[25]

But Batten also made another point: "The unhappy economic experiences of the recent past do not seem to have eroded the characteristic American desire to win. This survey leaves little doubt that Americans are unwilling to sit back and let other countries take economic initiatives away from us."[26] Precisely. By every available indicator, the American people are ready to be mobilized. A Penn-Schoen (Garth Analysis) poll taken in February 1983 phrased the issue slightly differently: "Some people say that America has permanently lost its position as the industrial leader of the world and some of its major industries will never compete in the world market again. Others say America's decline is only temporary and that we can continue to be the dominant economic force in the world. Which position is closer to your view?" Eighteen percent thought that America had permanently lost its industrial leadership, but 75 percent thought that the loss was only temporary.

Accordingly, the existence of a majority constituency within the business community and the public at large for a new activist agenda hardly seems in doubt. Protectionist anger is strong, but so is a more sophisticated nationalist preference for rebuilding America's competitive position by a new business-government partnership and a political and legal attack on unfair foreign trade practices.

Now for a specific approach.

CHAPTER
4

A Practical Agenda for
U.S. Industrial Competitiveness

My approach includes fifteen proposals—some specific, some general —grouped in five categories: (1) changes in federal trade organization, policy and law; (2) lobbying reform; (3) tax reform; (4) reform of labor-management relations; and (5) new efforts in education, research and technology.

Because mine is a political analysis of what can and should be done, I have not plumbed the depths of the various legal, economic and technological issues at stake, but have concentrated instead on questions of political strategy, the receptivity of public opinion, and a general sense of what approach may have a constituency and what probably does not. The final form of the agenda will emerge as a result of a process guaranteed to be highly political.

Some who may not take issue with my proposals may nevertheless argue that these recommendations do not have conservative support. Roughly two-thirds of them do, however, and a dozen are not out of kilter with the comments made by senior members of the Reagan administration during 1983 and 1984. Although the administration has repeatedly voiced its opposition to any form of industrial policy, its officials have nevertheless embraced enough related ideas—from establishment of a new federal Trade Department to trade reciprocity, antitrust reform, expansion of the Export-Import Bank, a shift of federal tax policy toward levies on consumption and multiple stimuli for technology—that we may already have a basis for a serious alternative federal strategy.

The major difference between the conservative and liberal views was apparent even before the 1984 election season got under way. The Republican administration's principal proposal was a new federal Department of International Trade and Industry, a nationalist ambition; the Democrats' principal response—which tactically they sought to interject into congressional consideration of the new Trade Department—was a national industrial planning council. Therein lies the deep cleavage: a new global assertion of U.S. economic interests versus a new degree of federal intervention in the structural arrangement and management of the domestic economy. Both trends have momentum. The political question lies in which one will dominate.

Meanwhile, and unfortunately for those who would like to run the economy from Washington, a considerable obstacle presents itself in the form of the federal system. The inchoate conservative strategy, emphasizing trade law and enforcement, new trade negotiations, federal export finance and modifications of federal antitrust and tax policies, does not in any real way trespass on the authority and pursuits of the fifty states. These, after all, are federal jurisdictional areas. Washington's action in these sectors will not stumble into the crazy-quilt regulations and statutes enacted by Harrisburg, Lansing, Jefferson City and Sacramento.

The same cannot be said of plans to sponsor chosen technologies from Washington or to ask federal agencies to coordinate industries operating in thirteen, thirty-four or even fifty states. Indeed, one great irony confronting federal industrial policy advocates is that for good, logical and highly political reasons, state after state has already begun to implement bits and pieces or even large chunks of state-level industrial policy. A federal Office of Technology Assessment spokesperson has observed that "the states are far ahead of the federal government in development of centers to help transfer technology from the entrepreneur or innovator to the market."[1] Half a dozen states have set up public corporations or boards for developing new products or funding new technologies. Roughly as many have passed laws requiring state public pension funds to serve as sources of capital for in-state investment. Dozens of states have been pondering their own export promotion units and even state foreign marketing boards. New Jersey's Republican Governor Thomas Kean has pioneered the concept of a state "infrastructure bank" to coordinate and finance state highway and transportation projects. Massachusetts' Democratic Governor Michael Dukakis notes, with only slight exaggeration, "While the national debate rages on whether we ought to have an industrial policy, there isn't a state that doesn't have one, or isn't putting one together, whether it has a Republican or Democratic, liberal or conservative governor."[2]

I won't say any more about state-level industrial policies save to note that their existence is both a political reality and an obstacle to federal planning ambition. The truth is that economic Balkanization and regionalization are a major force in the United States. Some of the fragmentation is benign and creative; some of it portends confusion, contradiction and inhibition of what may soon be necessary federal attempts to bring order out of steel or petrochemical industry redundancy. But however you interpret it, mushrooming state-level economic nationalism and mini-industrial policy are a fact of life in the 1980s, and that, coupled with basic Anglo-American skepticism of central government power—a tradition that simply does not lend itself to national planning—undercuts the practicality of major new national intervention in the economy, at least in the first stage of agenda setting.

In any case, I have put initial emphasis on a group of proposals for a tougher United States posture in international trade—from the creation of a Department of International Trade and Industry to expansion of the Export-Import Bank. This, parenthetically, is the most "conservative" portion of the competitiveness agenda. Virtually the entire list—with the exception of official commitment to fuller enforcement of existing trade laws—has been endorsed or embraced by the Reagan administration.

I go on to deal with ways to improve our trade politicking abroad while curbing the ability of foreign lobbyists to exploit trade-policy decision making in Washington. Though simple enough, this aspect of our policy and law enforcement weakness is often overlooked.

Tax policy also needs an overhaul. A special commission is the best solution. (This book will not, however, propose any new approaches to fiscal and monetary policy, even obvious ones like greater attention to a balanced budget or negotiation of new currency relationships with our trading rivals, especially Japan. Nothing could be more important, but it's the stuff of another volume, with political and constituency questions at once separate and enormously complicated. In any event, it's hard to see how better economic policy would undercut the case for any of my fifteen proposals.)

Also, attention must be paid to labor-management reform. Business and conservative agendas do not usually bring up the need, but they'll be in trouble if they don't recognize the issue.

Finally, I make a case for a national crash program in education, scientific research and technology. This is vital. Although many futurist notions of high tech are utopian and cannot be immediately realized, there's no doubt that we must embark on major initiatives to train a twenty-first-century work force and to maintain our jeopardized lead in basic research and technological innovation. Washington action against foreign industrial policies will count for naught unless we maintain and encourage Yankee ingenuity and human capital formation.

Below are listed the specifics for formulating a national competitiveness agenda.

A NEW DEPARTMENT OF TRADE

If we are to make competitiveness a national priority, nothing is more important than to create a new way to coordinate and elevate trade policy. The principal proposal, embraced by the Reagan administration in the summer of 1983, is to establish a federal Department of International Trade and Industry (DITI). Commerce Secretary Malcolm Baldrige, one of the idea's strongest backers, emphasized that "the making and implementation of trade policy will be under the same roof, and policy itself will be advocated, not brokered."[3] To date, of course, we have not seen that, because trade policy has been divided between the Commerce Department and the Office of the U.S. Trade Representative, with influential roles often played by various Cabinet departments. Critics are right when they say that the Treasury, State and Defense departments have often pursued separate goals—monetary, diplomatic or military—at the expense of trade considerations. Consider this rather flamboyant but also realistic commentary by Allegheny Ludlum Corporation President Richard Simmons:

> One of the great misconceptions in this country is that our government speaks with one voice. In the case of trade, particularly in the case of trade, it speaks with many voices, so many so that it speaks with no voice.

In any trade case involving a presidential decision, and this includes the very important Specialty Steel trade case decided by the President in July, let me walk you through the various outposts of influence.

First, it is necessary to understand that any trade case which would involve imposition of any trade restraint regardless of the nature of the restraint—or the justification—will be opposed by the State Department, the Treasury Department, Office of Management and Budget, Justice Department, and Council of Economic Advisors. In ten years, I do not know of a single trade case which was ever supported by any of the above-mentioned departments of government. Each department has its own justification for opposing relief of any kind. . . .[4]

To create a streamlined and effective organization, the new DITI would combine the Office of the U.S. Trade Representative with parts of the Commerce Department, among them the International Trade Administration, the Office of Economic Affairs, the National Telecommunications and Information Administration, and the Patent and Trademark Administration. The Reagan plan also called for a new Cabinet-level council to advise the President on trade and on the performance and competitive position of our economy.

Although many in Congress don't like the DITI idea, even skeptics have felt obliged to offer alternative proposals. Some have urged making the Commerce Department into an American equivalent of Japan's MITI. Others have suggested strengthening the U.S. Trade Representative's Office without merging it into the Commerce Department. Congressional Democrats, concerned with structural changes occurring with the internal U.S. economy, have proposed an economic coordinating council, which would help older basic industries and channel investment into emerging high-tech industries. Meanwhile, the Business–Higher Education Forum has advocated a new three-part scheme including a presidential adviser on economic competitiveness, a national commission on economic competitiveness and an information center on economic competitiveness in the Commerce Department.

Nevertheless, foreign precedents support Republican and business group insistence on a single, strong trade agency. That's the institutional mechanism most major Western nations have chosen, the most recent affirmation coming with British Prime Minister Margaret Thatcher's decision in 1983 to combine the previously separate ministries of trade and industry. Be it in London or Washington, coordina-

tion of domestic economic and trade policy has become critical.
Accordingly, the U.S. Chamber of Commerce, the American Business Conference and the National Association of Manufacturers
have endorsed the single-agency plan, and Lawrence Fox, the latter
group's Vice-President for International Economic Affairs, has underscored the logic of the arrangement.

> You hear the argument that the trade policymaking and negotiation responsibility has to be at the top, in the White House. Well,
> we've had it there, and it hasn't gotten us an effective Export-Import
> Bank. It hasn't found an answer to Japanese industrial targeting. No
> other government in the world would dismiss the overvalued dollar as an unfortunate minor side effect of budget deficits. If we had a
> strong Trade Department, Treasury wouldn't dominate exchange rate
> policy."[5]

These are precisely the considerations that validate Commerce
Secretary Baldrige's argument that "we cannot have a strong
trade policy without a strong, focused organization." Not even
the most sanguine observer thinks we have any such policy today.
On the contrary, organizational confusion and strategic disarray
have gone hand in glove. As tables 8 and 9 show, polling of U.S.
economists sponsored by the Japan Automobile Manufacturers
Association turned up an overwhelming belief that incoherent
trade policy has worked to create conflict with our trading partners.

As this is written, there is no polling evidence on whether Ameri-

TABLE 8.
Perceptions of U.S. Trade Policy

	All Respondents (%)	Academic Economists (%)	Business Economists (%)
A consistent overall trade policy	28	37	19
Various unintegrated policies but no coherent system	68	61	75
No real trade policy at all	4	2	6

SOURCE: 1983 Survey by Kane, Parsons, Inc., for Japan Automobile Manufacturers
Association, *JAMA FORUM*, vol. 1, no. 4 (1983).

TABLE 9.
*Perceptions of Effect of Lack of
Consistent U.S. Trade Policy*

	All Respondents* (%)	Academic Economists (%)	Business Economists (%)
Creates conflict with our trading partners	85	78	91
Not related to the state of our relations with our trading partners	8	12	5
Not sure	7	9	5

*Asked of those who replied that the United States has "no coherent system" or "no real trade policy at all" in the survey in table 8.

SOURCE: 1983 Survey by Kane, Parsons, Inc., for Japan Automobile Manufacturers Association, *JAMA Forum*, vol. 1, no. 4 (1983).

cans specifically favor the new Department of International Trade and Industry as proposed by the White House. Circumstantial survey evidence implies, however, that the public endorses a more assertive U.S. trade policy structure. A 1981 survey by Cambridge Reports found a national majority of 58 percent in favor of (with 21 percent against) "strengthening the U.S. government agencies responsible for developing long-term foreign trade policies and coordinating them with domestic economic policies."[6]

NEW TRADE-RECIPROCITY LEGISLATION

If we cannot afford to engage in outright protectionism—and we cannot—there is a plausible and moderate alternative: trade reciprocity. Few trade principles demonstrate more appeal to the U.S. electorate. Reciprocity, in a nutshell, means limited access to U.S. markets for any trading partner not allowing American products equal access in that nation's markets.* Given reciprocity, our trade officials would not be able to ignore complaints from U.S. manufacturers about foreign practices. Phone calls from the State Depart-

*The principal U.S. Senate architect of reciprocity legislation—International Trade Subcommittee Chairman John Danforth—stated as its purpose: "to achieve the same degree of access to foreign markets for competitive U.S. exports, services and investment as we accord to other countries" (*Congressional Record* 128 [11]: 5).

ment about "other considerations" would no longer work—or at least not as well. Our authorities would be required to monitor and assess foreign obstacles to U.S. exports—both products and services —and then take various forms of action and retaliation. This approach does, however, present some major problems. One difficulty is with the limitations that would need to be set—for example, what breadth of foreign market access earns what breadth of U.S. response? Nevertheless, it's hard to see how we can create enough leverage for sorely needed new trade negotiations without enacting some form of reciprocity first. (Parenthetically, discussion of reciprocity must also note the proposal for a new international legal framework for trade in services. Service industry executives support both that concept and the principle of bilateralism.)

As the data in tables 6 and 7 show, business executives strongly endorse reciprocity as a general policy guideline and—not surprisingly—so does the public. Results of an early 1983 poll done for the New York Stock Exchange found 76 percent of Americans supporting the basic idea that we should retaliate by imposing tariff and trade barriers on products being sold in the United States when foreign governments do the same to American goods.[7]

More substantiation can be found in a *Business Week*/Louis Harris sampling, taken in early 1983. Although the wording of Harris's question to some extent mixed apples (free trade) and oranges (reciprocity), *Business Week* summarized the results as follows: "Americans would still prefer a kind of loose reciprocal trade system to any plan that would restrict imports from Europe and Japan. And the preference is by an extremely large margin. Two-thirds of the national sample voted for fewer impediments to the free flow of goods, provided, of course, that U.S. exporters are treated liberally abroad."[8] The essential premise of people who back reciprocity legislation is that U.S. exporters are not so treated, and that new legal authority may be necessary to get the executive branch to apply the needed pressure.

This issue should soon enough appear front-and-center in national debate. A moderate form of trade-reciprocity legislation was reported from committee in the Senate in 1983 after supporting testimony was offered by administration spokesmen and by groups ranging from the U.S. Chamber of Commerce, the Business Roundtable and the National Association of Manufacturers to the Emergency Committee for American Trade.

FULL ENFORCEMENT OF EXISTING U.S. TRADE LAWS

During 1982 and 1983 the complaints of U.S. businessmen and labor leaders slowly grew into a roar. Washington, they said, was ignoring their protests about unfair foreign trade practices. Many of their complaints are legitimate. Part of the problem is that because trade policy making is so decentralized, foreign lobbyists have been able to shop around Washington for the best forum for their clients. They find an agency or department favorably disposed toward the hopeful foreign exporters. "Our competitors exploit our bureaucratic differences, as our own industries do," says Secretary Baldrige.[9] Meanwhile, U.S. trade law is also handicapped because of outdated provisions incapable of addressing new trade problems stemming from foreign government assistance to foreign exporters. Finally, when adequate protections for U.S. business *are* in the statute books, they are sometimes not enforced, because of the discretion legislation vests in the Office of the U.S. Trade Representative. That office has often not taken action after hearing domestic complaints, a pattern bluntly criticized, for example, in the comments of the 1983 report of the Labor-Industry Coalition for International Trade with regard to one key section (301) of U.S. trade law:

> Unlike the dumping or countervailing laws, section 301 contains a wide discretion and is administered directly by the President through the Office of the U.S. Trade Representative. The history of the implementation of this law, in part due to the discretion available and the direct role of the President, has been poor. This is the area of U.S. unfair trade law that offers the most potential for responding to the unfair trade effects of foreign industrial policies, yet it illustrates most clearly the ineffectiveness of granting broad discretion to the executive branch without a clear enough charge to defend U.S. commercial interests. Section 301 has provided almost no remedy for U.S. firms and workers unfairly disadvantaged by foreign government actions. . . . It is extraordinarily regrettable that the lesson of including discretion in trade laws is that the result is paralysis.[10]

Some new legislation is necessary, but nonenforcement of the existing law is also a political problem. In 1981 and 1982, U.S. Trade Representative Brock occasionally appeared to make light of trade law enforcement. Now he says: "Unless we fully enforce the dot and piddle—the small print—of the trade laws, we can't maintain a constituency for free international trade."[11] Nevertheless, outside pressures being what they are, some observers believe enforcement would be fuller if the Trade Representative's Office were absorbed by a new Department of International Trade.

In the meantime, there's no doubt whatever that the public favors tougher enforcement of existing trade laws. The 1981 Cambridge Reports survey made for Union Carbide found a 59-percent majority in favor of (with 18 percent against) "stricter enforcement of U.S. laws against dumped and subsidized imports, and the granting of temporary relief when import competition hurts U.S. industries."[12]

Parenthetically, there is also growing Washington interest in the idea of linking import relief to the requirement that protected industries modernize and become more efficient.

MONITORING FOREIGN INDUSTRIAL POLICIES AND NONTARIFF RESTRAINTS

There's widespread agreement here. In August 1982 the Commerce Department said it would begin to develop a data base on targeting practices of other governments.[13] Since then, numerous business groups and task forces have asked Washington to establish a serious effort to analyze the impact of foreign industrial policies and targeting practices. Most major business organizations endorsed related provisions in the Reciprocal Trade and Investment Act passed by the Senate in 1983.

By 1983, the Reagan administration was already experimenting in ad hoc ways to cope with foreign industrial policies. In May, Secretary Baldrige visited Japan to discuss that country's industrial policy and its effects on our economy. Speaking at the Japan Press Club, he said that the U.S. government will continue to give high priority to monitoring the shape and impact of Japanese industrial policy, saying that foreign industrial policy becomes "a matter of concern" when it spurs exports or limits imports of any country. Baldrige broached the idea that U.S. companies cooperate with Japanese firms and government agencies to sell in Japanese markets products, like petrochemicals, that Japanese companies cannot make at competitive prices. Baldrige went on to say that the Reagan administration hopes to propose a set of "international rules" to govern industrial policies.[14]

To be sure, some conservatives believe that foreign industrial policies in general—and Japan's in particular—are not a source of our competitive malaise. These conservatives assert that the United States does not need any industrial policy of its own and also that we don't need to pay much attention to foreign industrial policies. The ideological side of this debate can hardly be resolved by opinion polls, but in practical, political terms, survey data indicate that the public does indeed give considerable weight to the power of foreign governments in the international economy. In polling in 1981, Union Carbide asked the following question:

> Some people say that one of the reasons American companies have problems competing with foreign companies is that foreign governments either control or own these foreign companies. These people say this is unfair to American companies because these foreign companies get extra help from their governments and don't have to worry as much as American companies about earnings, profits and cutting costs. If you knew for a fact that this was true, do you think the U.S. should try to negotiate new rules of international trade that would make the competition between American companies and these firms fairer or not?[15]

With the question so phrased, 59 percent favored negotiations, 26 percent were not sure, and only 15 percent were opposed. On this issue, the public seems to agree with activist business groups who feel that it's about time to establish some new ground rules for industrial policies and international trade. A major world conference—a trade version of the 1945 Bretton Woods convocation that created the postwar monetary system—may be a good and necessary beginning.

PASSAGE OF LEGISLATION TO DEFINE UNFAIR TRADING PRACTICES, INCLUDING FOREIGN INDUSTRIAL POLICIES

At the moment existing international rules barely recognize and cannot govern the use of comprehensive industrial policies and targeting practices. Unfortunately, international negotiations to resolve this will obviously be long and difficult, as trade lawyers and diplomats can attest. So concerned business groups are asking Congress to amend our own trade laws to clarify the way American businesses can get trade relief against foreign industrial policies. The Labor-Industry Coalition for International Trade, in particular, urges "explicit recognition of industrial targeting as a type of action which constitutes 'a burden or restriction on U.S. commerce.' In other words, foreign industrial policies that target specific sectors for export growth in order to capture larger world market shares would be *per se* violations of U.S. unfair trade practices law.[16]

Valid objections can be offered to this position. Quantifying the "unfairness" of foreign industrial policies is going to be difficult, to say the least, and provocative. Since there are no international guidelines, legislation seeking to do this should be drafted slowly and carefully. But serious discussion is in order.

REVISION OF ANTITRUST POLICY TO SPUR DEVELOPMENT OF NEW TECHNOLOGIES

Our companies should be allowed to pool their efforts on research and development of new technologies. The real debate is about how far to go. From Atari Democrats to Reagan administration antitrust lawyers, support is growing for reinterpreting or amending our antitrust laws to let high-technology companies cooperate on certain dimensions to compete better in world markets. In September 1983 President Reagan proposed the "National Productivity and Innovation Act of 1983," which would provide, among other things, that the courts could find a joint research venture illegal only if actual U.S. anticompetitiveness effects outweigh global competitiveness merits.

Not surprisingly, the major spur to collaborative research has come from the microelectronics and computer technology sector. Across the Atlantic, the ten member nations of the European Community are looking at a joint plan called ESPRIT—European Strategic Program for Research in Information Technology—as their vehicle to catch up with the United States and Japan.[17] Meanwhile, fourteen major U.S. computer and electronics companies have banded together in a joint research consortium named MCC—the Microelectronics and Computer Technology Corporation—under a benign antitrust interpretation from the U.S. Justice Department. MCC will be working on the pure research side—developing processes and techniques that all member companies can share.

Such corporate joint research activities are almost certain to increase. At the same time, we must also make our concept of antitrust global. By such a standard, joint research efforts will be acceptable provided their sponsors do not control more than half of the world market. It's the global megamarket—no longer just the U.S. market alone—that would be the measure of things. So far, U.S. courts have not accepted the idea of a global market; getting them to do so is almost certainly a necessary point of policy departure in the new, internationalized (and internationally vulnerable) U.S. economy.

Consider several suggestions by LICIT. First, that U.S. authorities take action against collusive or anticompetitive behavior overseas by foreign companies that sell their products in the U.S. market: "Anti-competitive behavior which is not permitted for domestic firms selling in the domestic market should not be permitted for foreign firms exporting to the United States." And second, that the Justice Department take an expansive enough view to allow some forms of cooperation between domestic firms to facilitate their competition against foreign monopolies or cartels.[18] Our steel industry is the first obvious candidate. In 1983, Commerce Secretary Baldrige began urging an antitrust approach that would allow mature industries the flexibility to consolidate and strengthen themselves.

The American public backs the idea that industries should join hands to compete against foreigners. A Louis Harris survey made in 1981 for Sentry Insurance found 49 percent of the respondents backing (with 34 percent against) relaxation of the antitrust laws "to permit American companies to work together to compete more effectively in the world market."[19] Union Carbide's 1981 survey found 54 percent of the public favoring (and 23 percent against) an antitrust law exemption to allow large corporations to cooperate on foreign sales to give them an edge over foreign companies.[20]

TAX INCENTIVES AND IMPROVED EXPORT FINANCE

In addition to direct trade-law- and antitrust-law-related proposals, any serious national competitiveness strategy must include tax incentive and export credit improvements to enable U.S. firms to better contend with foreign rivals. For the time being, at least, it's expecting too much to assume that a group within the federal government can pick "winners and losers." But we should increase the availability of tax breaks and export assistance to industries competing with business-government partnerships in the global market. Expanded credit assistance for our exporters is especially critical. Industry after industry reports horror stories about how we have lost deals because we cannot match the competition of foreign (subsidized) export

financing packages. Figure 3 shows the gap in export financing between the United States and our major rivals.

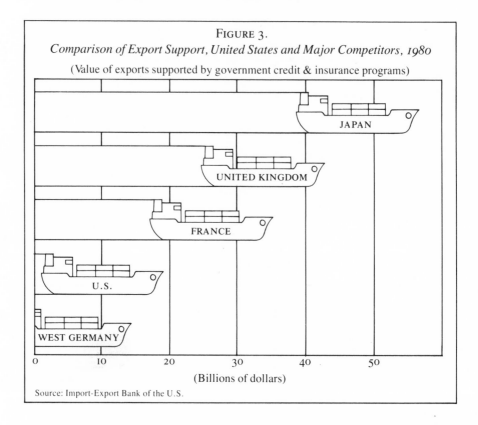

FIGURE 3.

Comparison of Export Support, United States and Major Competitors, 1980

(Value of exports supported by government credit & insurance programs)

JAPAN

UNITED KINGDOM

FRANCE

U.S.

WEST GERMANY

0   10   20   30   40   50

(Billions of dollars)

Source: Import-Export Bank of the U.S.

In the summer of 1983, the Coalition for Employment through
Exports, a group of labor unions, state governors and corporations
(including General Electric, Allis-Chalmers and Fluor), convinced
the Reagan administration to support an increase in the Export-
Import Bank's lending authority as well as to implement a new
language in the bank's charter directing it to counter aggressively
credit subsidies offered by foreign governments.[21] The measure was
signed into law in late 1983, but it's only a start. More Export-Import
Bank credit is still needed.

Contrary to rhetoric proclaiming voter unwillingness to back
"corporate subsidies," public opinion is broadly supportive. Based
on surveys made between 1981 and 1983, Americans favor giving tax
breaks and subsidies to companies that compete with subsidized

foreign companies (49 percent for, 43 percent against; Louis Harris/ *Business Week*, 1982); 54 percent support (with 30 percent against) "tax incentives for U.S. manufacturing and service industries to compete abroad" (Cambridge Reports/Union Carbide, 1981); they favor federal subsidies for U.S. products to make them more competitive with Japanese products (by 57 percent, in 1983 Los Angeles *Times* polling); and they endorse increased support of U.S. exports through low-interest loans provided by the Export-Import Bank in order to compete with foreign low-interest loans (59 percent for, 21 percent against; Cambridge Reports/Union Carbide, 1981).[22]

STRONG OVERSEAS LOBBYING ARMS AND TIGHTENED U.S. LOBBYING LAWS

There is no doubt that lobbying and influence-peddling are major factors in relative national trade competitiveness. High among the priorities of a new trade policy should be a concerted effort to do away with multiple U.S. naïveté. On the one hand, U.S. exports suffer from the way in which our businessmen are blocked by U.S. law from taking advantage, while overseas, of the looser business and ethical practices of foreign nationals; and, on the other, the United States, in turn, brings virtually no regulation to bear on the massive expenditures made by Washington lobbyists of foreign governments and corporations eager to manipulate—one could even say corrupt—American trade policy.

In the first instance, business groups have been restrained in their criticism of the 1977 Foreign Corrupt Practices Act, passed in the heyday of moral righteousness just after Watergate. The legislation's net impact, however, has been to proscribe all sorts of minor expenditures Congress never intended to ban, and to impose inordinately expensive accounting practices. Trade Representative William Brock has testified before Congress that the law has cost U.S. industry billions of dollars in sales and thousands of jobs. Economist Lawrence Krause of the Brookings Institution blames the law for much of the business lost to the Japanese in developing nations like the Philippines and Indonesia.[23] In 1983, Congress took up modifications to give U.S. corporations more leeway in making "any expenditures, including travel and lodging expenses, associated with the selling or purchasing of goods and services. . . ." Bluntly put, American exporters, when in Rome, should be allowed to do as the Romans do.

Something else is also in order. Besides sharpening their overseas business practices, U.S. corporations have to begin to apply in foreign capitals the sort of lobbying skills that foreigners, especially the Japanese, have brought to bear in Washington during the last decade. In April 1983, Robert C. Angel, president of the Japan Economic Institute of America, told a Midwestern business conference that our businessmen should immediately set up an information and lobbying organization in Tokyo "that would be the eyes, ears and mouth of American business."[24] Lack of any such operation today clearly leaves a vacuum. Individual company offices in Tokyo are there simply to conduct business, and the U.S. embassy cannot play a lobbying role. As Angel put it, "I think we have to move to work inside their system, do the grubby things that other countries do in Washington. What I'm talking about is what is euphemistically called in Washington 'government affairs activities.' Translated into English, that means lobbying."

To implement this strategy, Angel suggested an organization funded by a consortium of U.S. firms and headed by a well-known, respected figure. Buttressing that operation should be an effort to gather information and "to conduct the public affairs program of American business in Japan," as Angel puts it.

More to the point is that if we are to recapture control of our own trade policy formulation and administration, we are going to have to crack down on the foreign lobbyists in general—and the Japanese lobbyists and agents in particular—who swarm in Washington like bees around a honeypot.

In 1980, according to a Chicago *Tribune* survey, hired Americans reported earning a whopping $196 million from foreign clients for trying to influence U.S. policy and public opinion.[25] An analysis by *U.S. News & World Report* in 1982 found the expanding use of direct lobbying by foreign governments and industries beginning to worry lawmakers. "So much money is available that it's corrupting our governmental system," observed the late U.S. Congressman Benjamin Rosenthal, chairman of the Investigations Subcommittee of the House Government Operations Committee. "Foreign powers are able to hire very distinguished Americans with fine records to do their bidding—frequently when those interests are contrary to American interests."[26]

In Michigan, the Detroit *News* put the issue a bit less genteelly: "The largest and best-financed army of lobbyists in Washington marches under the flag of the land of the Rising Sun. Scores of lawyers and lobbyists—many of them former federal officials now drawing six-figure salaries—are supplying legal counsel, information and influence for the government industrial complex known informally as Japan, Inc. Their mission: to prevent erosion of Japan's trade dominance over the United States."[27] In 1977, when the U.S. trade deficit with Japan was only $1.5 billion, Japan had only seventeen registered agents in Washington. But by the time 1982 rolled around, the U.S. trade deficit with Japan had climbed to $25 billion —and Japan had over a hundred registered lobbyists.

The Detroit *News* quoted a Justice Department lawyer who handles antitrust matters involving the Japanese as saying that "there are hundreds of [other] people in Washington's most prestigious legal, consulting and public relations firms who are paid six-figure salaries by the Japanese to work quietly behind the scenes to help them retain present trade advantages. . . . I'd estimate that Japan will spend at least $200 million this year on its campaign to keep the status quo in its trading relations with the United States—and that's a very conservative estimate."[28]

Others have said the same thing to media outside Michigan—and for the record. In 1982, the Chicago *Tribune* quoted Trade Representative Brock as saying, "It is true that the Japanese particularly have sought to employ every public affairs and lobbying expert in this town."[29] Joe Clarkson, chief of enforcement for the Justice Department's Foreign Agent Registration Branch (FARB), told the *Tribune* that the Japanese "are much more ambitious than the others" about hiring well-connected Americans to advise them and intercede for them. "They think nothing about hiring two American firms and giving them both the same assignment so they can compare the advice they get. I remember one case when they commissioned reports from two separate places to advise them on the impact Koreagate [a congressional bribery scandal] would have on Japanese lobbying programs."[30]

Incidentally, FARB officials underscore one revealing fact—that the Japanese prefer to hire people who have worked in the U.S. Trade Representative's Office in Washington. Yet they are almost as interested in individuals with high-level political connections, men like Democratic National Chairman Charles T. Manatt (whose law firm has represented Japanese interests) and former Reagan campaign manager John Sears. Others who work for the Japanese include former National Security Adviser Richard Allen and former CIA Director William Colby. Trade policy influence comes in many packages.

The Detroit *News* quotes an American executive connected to the Washington office of a large Japanese corporation as saying, "When it comes to lobbying the government, the Japanese have their American competitors beat five ways to one. Money is no object to them. They hire the best and they do so on a bipartisan basis. Nobody's going to investigate them because they've got both parties locked up."[31]

This does not overstate matters much. In fact, if any serious tightening of the federal lobbying law—currently riddled with loopholes—occurs, it will measure how much economic nationalism here has already developed.

TAX POLICIES TO SPUR INTERNATIONAL COMPETITIVENESS

The formulation of U.S. tax strategy must take into account the need to stay competitive globally. And probably the best way to develop new tax approaches is for the President to appoint a blue-ribbon commission to report in a nonelection year, by which point Congress might be ready to grapple with ideas that would be given short shrift or thrown aside in a context more charged politically.

Charls Walker, chairman of the American Council for Capital Formation and former Deputy Secretary of the Treasury, has proposed such a commission, hoping that it would recommend a shift to taxation of consumption rather than of income or capital formation. His preferred position on new tax policy—and the preference of others ranging from former Council of Economic Advisers Chairman Alan Greenspan on the right to economist Lester Thurow on the left—is a value-added tax (VAT). Increasingly relied upon in Europe, VAT has emerged as a vehicle for raising large sums of revenue without increasing the tax burden on income savings or capital formation. VAT refundability where goods are sold overseas can of course benefit exporters. Treasury Secretary Donald Regan concurs with the need for tax reform: "If U.S. industry is to remain competitive, not only with other industrial nations but with advanced developing countries, it probably will be necessary to move toward consumption taxes."[32]

Two other ideas proposed by business groups should also receive a hearing from any commission. The first is adjustment of capital gains taxes to account for inflation, as proposed by the Committee for Economic Development. Because the public approves of indexing, this idea could well be salable. Second, the American Business Conference proposes making preferred dividends paid by corporations tax-deductible. That's not the case now, of course. The supporting argument rests on the idea that our corporations raise money for expansion by selling stock rather than by obtaining bank loans, unlike Japanese and many other foreign corporations. For global competitiveness, the dividend payments are really a form of interest expense. But whereas the Japanese interest payments are tax-deductible, the dividend payments by U.S. corporations are not. The competitive implications are just what one might expect—and then some. Look at figure 4, which shows the real cost of capital in the United States versus its cost in Japan, based on an American Business Conference report.

According to Massachusetts electronics executive George Hatsopoulos, who supervised the preparation of the American Business Conference report, making dividend payments tax-deductible would

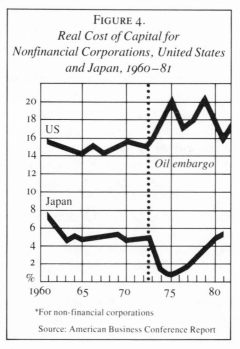

FIGURE 4.
Real Cost of Capital for
Nonfinancial Corporations, United States
and Japan, 1960–81

*For non-financial corporations

Source: American Business Conference Report

lower the real cost of U.S. capital to around 9 percent, within three points of the Japanese cost. At that level, the United States' long-term competitive chances become formidable once again.[33]

In sum, the three most useful reforms in the U.S. tax system would be: (1) a value-added tax; (2) federal capital gains adjustment for inflation; (3) federal corporate income tax deductibility for payment by corporations of preferred dividends.

RESTRUCTURED LABOR-MANAGEMENT RELATIONS

Even though left-of-center industrial policy advocates overstate the degree to which Japanese or German industry is one big happy family, old-line adversarial labor-management relationships in fact greatly undercut U.S. competitiveness. Senior executives of major corporations realize that, whatever the merits of right-to-work laws in Idaho or Oklahoma, the trend in the older, endangered, heavily unionized heavy industries lies in the direction of increased business-labor cooperation. Unless the old Anglo-American tradition of adversiality is replaced by a new and collaborative relationship, productivity and quality-of-work gains will be difficult to achieve. And automation—in many industries the only hope of successful U.S. international competition—will suffer.

Several recent surveys suggest that Americans have a strong commitment to the work ethic but that present management attitudes and circumstances in the workplace undermine that commitment. American workers do not feel involved, nor do they believe they will profit from performance or productivity gains. To remedy this, workers must feel they have a stake, and the government must encourage more companies to embrace the approaches being pioneered in the automobile industry, where progress has been considerable. In 1981 Chrysler became the first major U.S. corporation to appoint a union chief—Douglas Fraser, at the time president of the United Auto Workers—to its board. General Motors' new plant in Wentzville, Missouri, combines the most modern technology with extensive worker training and Japanese management techniques in a bid to revolutionize U.S. auto manufacturing. Employees are trained to get along with one another and with the computer. Workers participate in decisions ranging from establishing job assignments to what tools the company will buy for the assembly line, as discussion groups and quality-of-work programs are being established at all levels. William J. Usery, former Secretary of Labor in the Ford administration and a consultant to General Motors, says, "We're talking about building a whole new workplace." He also talks about developing a "non-adversarial relationship" with the United Auto Workers.[34]

In a similar vein, Secretary of Labor Raymond Donovan has understood "that in this economic world, this global village that we live in called the world, there is a war going on, for jobs. It puts pressure on management, puts pressure on labor, and the positive thing I am beginning to see as I go around the country is a dawning recognition that labor and management have to see themselves as economic partners, as allies, with an attitude of cooperation rather than confrontation."[35] Coming from a New Right favorite, those words suggest a growing conservative ideological flexibility on the issue of labor-management relations. When Republican labor secretaries use this language, local chambers of commerce should—and will—listen.

Moreover, a growing number of business organizations already back the idea of collaborating with labor. The Committee for Economic Development's 1983 study *Productivity Policy: Key to the Nation's Future* recommended a host of innovations ranging from a joint management-labor effort to reshape work rules to gain-sharing systems, quality circles and labor-management participation teams. And LICIT, in its 1983 report on coping with foreign industrial policies, observed:

> The experience of the Steel Tripartite Committee from 1978 to 1980 offers positive lessons on the potential for labor-management-government cooperation in finding solutions for problems facing individual American industries. More broadly, cooperative efforts by industry and labor, such as the Labor-Industry Coalition for International Trade, have convinced those of us involved that an often surprisingly broad range of consensus exists (or can be developed) among labor, management and government on issues affecting the future of American industry.[36]

Even bolder analyses and proposals are coming from individual corporate chief executive officers. In a speech to the Philadelphia World Affairs Council in June 1983, Eastern Airlines Chairman Frank Borman said, "The question mark that is out today is whether the airline industry or the auto industry or the steel industry can make the transition, to accept the fact that labor is now part of the competitive picture."[37] Borman believes that wages should be linked to industry profits and that employees should have seats on the board of directors. At Aetna, Chairman John Filer has proposed appointment of a national commission on human capital.[38] At General Foods, President Philip L. Smith has suggested that the work environment offers the next major threshold for productivity advancement: "I believe that the next big productivity advance will come through better utilization of people." He adds that individuals both in management and on the production line "really don't work anywhere near their potential as human beings—not because they don't want to, but because we give them a working environment that denies them satisfaction. Finding a working environment that gives them that satisfaction will produce real productivity benefits for us."[39]

During the last two decades, as American business, labor and government went their unmerry and uncoordinated ways, U.S. productivity has deteriorated relative to the gains chalked up in countries where business, labor and government work together. Figure 5 shows the trend. Note that the greatest productivity gains occurred in the three countries that are the leading practitioners of industrial policy.

Poll data confirm that both the general public and opinion leaders endorse a new business-labor-government collaborative approach. A survey released in the summer of 1983 by New Jersey's Opinion Research Corporation showed a vast majority of elites in all fields favoring "industrial modernization agreements"—tripartite commitments: by management to modernize plants, expand research and development and retrain workers; by government to provide targeted tax and import relief; and by labor to accept wages tied to productivity. Of the opinion leaders polled, 75 percent endorsed the concept of an industrial modernization agreement; this endorsement came from 71 percent of the business executives, 71 percent of the union leaders and 81 percent of the elected government officials.[40]

In August 1983 the Reagan administration reestablished the joint government-industry-labor advisory committee to look into ways of revitalizing the steel industry. In some industries, such a tripartite committee can perhaps pave the way to tripartite agreements.

Obviously, improved management-labor relations are not the only key to productivity, but the two are closely linked.

FIGURE 5.
Manufacturing Productivity Growth,
United States and Major Competitors, 1960–81

(For each country, 1960 equals 100)

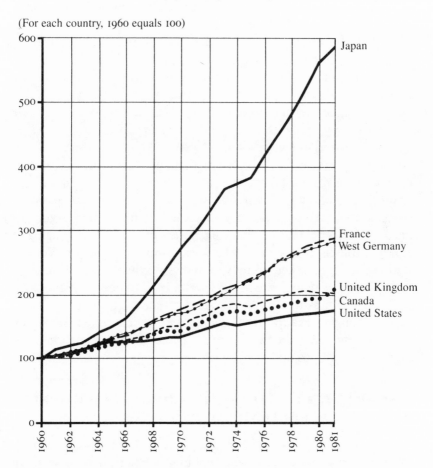

This graph compares the increase in each nation's manufacturing productivity from 1960 to 1981. It does not show relative levels of overall productivity.

Source: Committee for Economic Development

MECHANISMS FOR MONITORING INDUSTRIAL PLANT CLOSINGS

Given the vicissitudes of the global marketplace, protection for business and protection for labor must to some extent go hand in hand. The changing global economy, the decline of U.S. basic industries, and ongoing high unemployment in America have led the AFL-CIO in a number of Northern industrial states to push for plant-closing legislation—statutes requiring corporations to give six to twelve months' notice of plans to shut down factories or to reduce their work force by more than a certain percentage. The arguments against this kind of legislation on the state level are considerable, to be sure. Businesses will think twice about starting or expanding operations in places having such constraints. Yet a certain amount of protection along these lines for workers—and for their unions—seems a necessary political component of any new business-government-labor partnership. Requiring notice of planned closings and major layoffs is pretty much the norm among our major Western trade competitors. Accordingly, it seems inevitable that similar attempts must be made here at the federal level to deal with the same problem. Perhaps we should pay some attention to the general success of Canada's Manpower Consultative Service, which becomes a party to discussions in an advisory capacity after notification of an intended plant closing.[41]

FEDERAL LEGISLATION FOR A DISPLACED-WORKER RETRAINING PROGRAM

Everyone agrees that the United States has to develop a new technologically trained work force. But not everyone agrees on how much retraining of members of today's low-tech work force should or may cost. Politically, however, a large-scale retraining effort seems obligatory, because it will demonstrate to the international community that we are committed to being competitive, substitute for or supplement welfare and unemployment support, and reassure apprehensive blue-collar Americans.

Yet there's no consensus here. Among business groups only a few have come out for a massive national retraining program. One such supporter is the Business–Higher Education Forum, which has endorsed the equivalent of a GI bill for displaced workers. In large measure, this approach draws on the views of Patrick Choate, senior economic policy analyst for the TRW Corporation, who argues that the United States is already beginning to encounter what he feels will become an enormous problem. As automation comes into industry after industry during the 1980s and early 1990s, millions of Americans now employed in manufacturing will lose their jobs. Technology will leave human tragedy in its wake unless a major national retraining commitment is made—and made now, for the long term.

Choate's remedy? A "single, coherent, comprehensive national displaced worker training program" to be funded by workers and employers, with government involved only to collect and audit the money spent. Individual training accounts financed by payroll taxes would pay for the retraining of future displaced workers.[42]

Choate is right to say that we lack a policy approach for dealing with massive structural unemployment. "We really don't have any institutions, structures or policies for training or retraining the adults. We have said if you are out of a job, you need help, and if you have a job, you don't. We could get by with that up until this decade. But those days are gone forever."[43] The trouble is, a large part of the business community doesn't like his remedy. For starters, many people doubt whether high-tech and industrial automation—the coming of the job-killing robots—will proceed as far during the 1980s as futurists predict. The Congressional Budget Office, for one, predicts that three million jobs—15 percent of the current manufacturing work force—could be lost by 1990 in older industries, especially in automobiles and steel.[44] By contrast, the federal Bureau of Labor Statistics, in its most recent projections, concludes that the percentage of decline in manufacturing has come to a virtual halt, and that the number of manufacturing jobs will actually rise by up to five million in this decade.[45] Given disagreement of that magnitude, small wonder there's no consensus about what to do.

There is also reason to doubt the effectiveness of any massive job retraining program. A survey made by the Urban Institute suggests, for example, that workers who lose jobs in declining industries are no more likely to become structurally unemployed than workers who lose jobs in expanding industries.[46] Yet another problem with retraining Rust Bowl workers is that few local slots are available in jobs for which they can be retrained—and older employees don't want to relocate. Finally, it is estimated that business already spends some $30–50 billion a year on employee training, doing a reasonably good, though nationally uncoordinated, job.[47]

Under the circumstances, it's no surprise that no consensus exists in the business community for any major new federal retraining effort beyond the Reagan administration's $4-billion-a-year Job Training Partnership Act, signed in 1982. This legislation relies on business-oriented councils around the country to evaluate local situations as well as to develop—and operate—any retraining programs found necessary. The responsibility rests with business, and, for the moment, business wants to keep it. Robert Craig, executive director of the American Society for Training Directives, says that his group is reluctant to back any proposal that involves government deeply, because the incentive and the work should come from the employee and the employer: "They have a job to get done, and they do it far better than public education. We think you need accountability in job training. The person who has to get the production done ought to be responsible for the quality of the training."[48]

Fair enough. But I'm also inclined to agree with a less sanguine thesis advanced by *Fortune* magazine editor A. F. Ehrbar, who feels that major worker displacement in manufacturing is possible, and the best case for a larger retraining program may be political, not economic. "If retraining can help lay the ghost of Ned Ludd [the nineteenth-century Englishman who led his followers to smash new machinery] and reduce the clamor for quotas (protectionism), it will be one of the more tolerable political pay-offs."[49]

FEDERAL SUPPORT FOR TECHNOLOGICAL RESEARCH AND DEVELOPMENT

Encouraging technology without stifling innovation won't come easily for politicians ill-at-ease with silicon as a new industrial art form. Corporate executives are also ambiguous. For the most part, U.S. businessmen—not least venturers in high-technology fields—oppose establishment of a federal agency to identify and fund promising high-tech industries facing intense competition from abroad. As one venture capitalist puts it, "Technological innovation is a many-flowered and often accidental process." Nolan Bushnell, the founder of Atari, has observed that a federal panel would never have picked Atari for development as a competitive industry.

What business does want is greater indirect government assistance through increased federal backing for research and development.

Foremost on the list is permanent status for the federal tax credit for research and development enacted in 1981. Beyond that, there are many other suggestions. The New England Council, for example, suggests a multiple approach. The group favors tax incentives to encourage the private sector to support the development of scientific and engineering education, and it proposes other incentives to ensure continued availability of risk capital for R&D. And they also want a "Basic Research Trust Fund," which, they hope, can remove federal money for basic research from the annual vagaries of budget making.[50] Meanwhile, the Committee for Economic Development suggests full, rather than partial, funding of basic research by universities under government contract. No serious competitiveness agenda can proceed without commitments to several of these proposals.

NEW SAFEGUARDS AGAINST TECHNOLOGY TRANSFER, ESPIONAGE AND THEFT

Many experts worry about the way our technological lead is being dissipated by transfer—or theft—of technology. As the Washington *Post* noted in a recent survey, Japanese companies obtained most of the world's available advanced technology between 1950 and 1980 by signing at least 30,000 licensing or technical agreements with major companies, mostly American, and "the price paid by Japan in royalties and fees has been about $10 billion, less than one-fifth of what is spent in the United States for research and development in one year."[51] Of course, technology exchange is a two-way street. The United States gets as well as gives technology—not least from and to Japan. Overall, though, it's appropriate to pay increased attention to the question of safeguarding technology, as well as to its research and development.

In May 1983 the New York *Times* reported that a year-old federal program to restrict the export of sophisticated U.S. technology had begun to cut into the loss of industrial secrets to foreign countries. Nevertheless, "attempts by the Soviet Union, France, Japan, China, Israel and other countries to obtain U.S. technology are so pervasive and safeguards for protecting industry are so porous that the United States is losing its technological edge through espionage, legitimate sales and American greed."[52] In June 1983, the Investigations Subcommittee of the House Committee on Energy and Commerce held hearings on the loss of our industrial secrets and charged that foreign competitors are stealing billions of dollars' worth of information with little more than a mere slap for punishment. Congressman Edward Markey of Massachusetts suggested that "Congress will have to pass tough new laws and the U.S. government will have to have tough talks with governments such as the Japanese . . . to show that the American public has little tolerance for this sort of activity."[53] His point is hardly arguable.

Copyright protection, too, is a growing area of U.S. concern. Japan's Ministry of International Trade and Industry, anxious to nurture and protect Japanese software developers, has been blue-printing new legal approaches that would give MITI itself the authority to force a company to license its software to another should the government deem such action to be in the national interest. Reacting to MITI's early 1984 proposal, Vico Henriques, president of the U.S. Computer & Business Equipment Manufacturers Association (CBEMA), deplored it as a vehicle for industrial piracy: "This would allow them to raid the developed software around the world."[54]

Patent relations between the United States and Japan are also a problem, according to many analysts. Back in 1960, Americans applied for many more patents than did the Japanese, but now the pattern has reversed. In 1982, Japan's electronics industry filed more than 10,000 patents in the microelectronics field, and this year the number is expected to reach 18,000—twice the number of microelectronics-related patent applications in the United States and four times the rate in West Germany. This despite the fact that the U.S. semiconductor industry, which will be most affected by the patents, is twice as large as Japan's. As reported in a major analysis by the Dallas *News*, Fumoi Wada of the International Technology Group, a market research firm, underscores that the Japanese often file for patents only in Japan, not overseas, in order not to have to make the details of their technological advances public.[55] Japanese patent information must be published, to be sure, but only in Japanese. For that reason, U.S. firms and agencies tend not to stay abreast. As for their own filing of patents overseas, some Japanese firms take that so seriously, according to Wada, that they have standing committees to make these weighty decisions. Meanwhile, when it comes to monitoring the open U.S. patent system, the Japanese are highly organized: "Companies such as Hitachi and Mitsubishi have more than 100 technical librarians whose job it is to gather technological information from around the world and sort it and file it for the company."

Curtis Landi, president of Patent Research Associates, in Palo Alto, argues: "The Japanese have been successful in the electronics industry not because of their engineering capabilities, but because of their appreciation of what's in patents."[56] Moreover, the newly developed countries of East Asia—Korea, Singapore and Malaysia—have all learned from the Japanese; and Taiwan, because it is no longer recognized under international law as a nation, is not constrained by international patent law.

Current patent law, like the related problems of technology transfer and high-tech espionage, calls out for modification and reform. Slowness in carrying ideas and known technology into commercial success is one of the weakest links in America's manufacturing process. Other nations wind up getting the benefit of American research and innovation. As of 1984, both Commerce Secretary Malcolm Baldrige and John Young, president of Hewlett-Packard and chairman of the President's Commission on Industrial Competitiveness, have urged increased attention to patents and to improvement of the patent laws to safeguard U.S. intellectual property.

EDUCATION FOR ECONOMIC DEVELOPMENT, JOB CREATION AND NATIONAL DEFENSE

A greatly increased emphasis on education is well on its way to becoming part of the new American consensus. Politicians, public opinion polls, business organizations and just about everyone else feel that we cannot compete without a better educational system. In May 1983 the National Task Force on Education for Economic Growth reported as follows:

> Approximately 95 percent of Japanese teen-agers now graduate from high school versus 74 percent in the United States. Because Japan's schools are in session five and a half days a week, and because the Japanese school year is longer than ours, the typical Japanese high school graduate has the equivalent of roughly four full years more than an American high school graduate. . . .
>
> If we are serious about economic growth in America—about improving productivity, about recapturing competitiveness in our basic industries and maintaining it in our newer industries, about guaranteeing to our children a decent standard of living and a rewarding quality of life, then we must get serious about improving education. And we must start now.[57]

As might be expected, an array of groups—business, academic and hybrid—have made many suggestions for such improvement. At the state level, new incentives to foster math and science education are being offered, such as scholarships, bonuses, student loan rebates and the like. States anxious to court high-tech industries are putting new emphasis on research parks and university clusters. In Texas, the Dallas *News* ran a major analysis of education that was headlined "Dallas, Inc., Must Get Smart."[58]

But here, too, a major push must come at the federal level. And it must measure up to the growing public demand for a national mobilization for competitiveness. Probably the most appropriate solution lies in a proposal by Ray Stata, chief executive officer of Analog Devices and former president of the Massachusetts High Technology Council (MHTC), for a contemporary high-tech equivalent of the Morrill Act, which established land-grant colleges dedicated to research and education in agriculture.* In a January 1983 speech to an MHTC meeting attended by President Reagan, Stata called for a partnership of industry, academia and government to target the aims of education on economic development, job creation and national defense, "and to build centers of technical excellence throughout the country. . . . Specifically," he continued, "we are proposing a matching grant program, for technical education and research where industry goes first in putting its money on the line. Next, state government should verify the benefits of industry's investment by its own matching grants. After industry, academia and state government have agreed, we need Uncle Sam to do his part in the participating as well."[59]

Considering the state of U.S. public opinion, nothing less than a major thrust in technological education—surpassing the one used to mobilize Americans after Russia took the lead with Sputnik in 1957 —will be acceptable. Because the nation is ready to rally behind an effort to regain economic competitiveness, no serious agenda can be without a new and significant commitment to education.

OUTLINES OF A COMPETITIVENESS CONSENSUS

Somewhere within these positions, I think there is a viable U.S. competitiveness agenda—part high-tech optimism, part traditional

---

*Introduced as legislation in 1983 by Massachusetts Democratic Senator Paul Tsongas.

liberal interventionism, part conservative nationalism and inclination to maximize free-market reliance, and part business-community moderation, synthesis, pragmatism and sheer commercial expertise.

If liberal approaches are more ambitious, the odds are that they don't make much sense politically. Free-market conservatives often exaggerate the merits of unfettered economic competition, but they are right when they say that liberal economic interventionist agendas are often less concerned with economics per se and more with intervention per se. David Warsh, of the Boston *Globe,* a former *Forbes* magazine editor and one of America's most perceptive economic journalists, observed that most advocates of a national industrial policy have ignored the serious proposals made and steps taken by business groups. He was talking specifically about the innovative MCC research consortium, a private organization launched by high-tech companies. Control Data, based in Minneapolis, took the lead in founding it, the Justice Department provided a sufficient antitrust law dispensation, and Texas private enterprise provided critical funding. As Warsh noted, "MCC is no MITI yet, but it has growth potential. Interestingly, though, it has stirred very little enthusiasm among many of the innovative liberal thinkers who have been most vocal in calling for industrial planning. Perhaps because it involves no heavy federal role in targeting of projects, MCC has been ignored by investment banker-planner Felix Rohatyn, economist Lester Thurow, Barry Bluestone of Boston College and MIT's Harley Shaiken. All of them declined to comment on the subject."[60]

All the more reason why an industrial competitiveness strategy that is more enterprise-oriented has a very good chance to make it in the real world; its agenda is already generally agreed upon. The case for my fifteen points is reasonably solid. The case for the federal intervention desired by the left is not. The latter approach has not been disproved, but nevertheless it remains unproved. Meanwhile, reforms backed by consensus should be pursued first. For many Americans, even these will mark a watershed in government's economic role.

CHAPTER
5

Conservative Traditions of Economic Intervention

The laissez-faire conservative's view of the role of government is simply inadequate in today's global economy. To have any real impact on the debate about competitiveness, conservatives are going to have to do two things: first, look to the conservative activism in Western Europe and Japan; and second, draw on the example of business-government partnership in the early days of our own republic. These precedents and examples ought to be intriguing, if not compelling.

U.S. BUSINESS NATIONALISM FROM 1790 TO 1840

Few Americans know that the first stage of the industrial revolution in the United States—the half-century from 1790 until about 1840—was one that featured intensive government participation and intervention in economic development. Moreover, those with conservative views (the political allies of the business and financial classes did not begin to use the term "conservative" until the 1830s) were the principal sponsors of the collaboration.

Although this is not a history text, I'd like to talk for a moment about our past. It is important to know that conservative economics has not always meant what it means now. Not at all. Most signers of the Declaration of Independence and the architects of the Constitution were at home with the idea of state economic activism. The man usually credited with being the source of their philosophic inspiration, the seventeenth-century English philosopher John Locke, took state activity for granted in his views of economics, since more than a little mercantilism colored his outlook. William Letwin, in his *Origins of Scientific Economics*, notes that Locke was not "inclined to go to the length of suggesting *laissez-faire* in the range of economic policy. Quite the contrary. The state papers he composed while a Commissioner for Trade—especially his famous proposal to suppress the woollen manufacture of Ireland and replace it with linen—as well as the repeated insistence in the *Considerations* that the government must regulate trade in order to assure a proper balance of trade: these show he was very much an advocate of government intervention in economic affairs."[1]

Alexander Hamilton, the first U.S. Secretary of the Treasury, architect of the U.S. financial system and deemed by many to be the new nation's first conservative political theorist, was a notable interventionist. One biographer, Professor Richard Morris, describes Hamilton's views as follows:

> Believing as he did in a government possessed with energy and initiative, he could scarcely be expected to allow the government to stand inert while the economy stagnated or was stifled by foreign competition. Hamilton advocated a nationally directed and controlled economy in the interest of private enterprise. He believed that the economy should be invigorated and protected by bounties and tariffs, by canals, roads and other improvements built by the federal government. . . . Hamilton's Report ("Report on the Subject of Manufactures," 1791) stands as the bible of advocates of government aid to encourage industry.[2]

The views of Hamilton, in turn, foreshadowed those of Henry Clay, Daniel Webster and the Whig Nationalists of the pre–Civil War period. Clay and Webster advocated the "American System" of federally financed internal improvements—their version of the transportation "infrastructure," now the subject of so much political attention. They also advocated subsidy and protection of our industries, as well as a national bank—the controversial Second Bank of the United States partly owned by the federal government—to ensure a sound currency.

The government activism coincided with a proliferation of corporate charters. Prior to 1790, few corporations existed in the new United States and fewer had existed in the colonies. But between 1790 and 1800, the number of corporations chartered by the first sixteen states increased from 37 to 344, many of them for building turnpikes, bridges and canals.[3] A second surge came during the War of 1812, when according to Harvard Law School's late Professor E. Merrick Dodd, "some state governments appeared to have adopted the view that the chartering of domestic manufacturing associations was a matter of patriotism."[4] The point to remember here is that corporations, specially chartered by state legislatures, were chips off the block of sovereignty, created because of a political decision to allow or participate in a specific economic enterprise. Corporate activity in the early nineteenth century represented government economic activism almost by definition.

As Stanford Professor Lawrence M. Friedman puts it in his *A History of American Law*:

> State partnership in corporate enterprise seemed natural in the early 19th century. In the first place, many corporations were chartered to do work traditionally part of the function of the state. These jobs included road building, banking and the digging of canals. Secondly, since each franchise was a privilege and favor, the state had the right to exact a price, which might include strict control or even profit sharing. Thirdly, state participation was a good way to help out an enterprise. It was a way of priming the pump, a way of supporting vital enterprise that would in turn enliven the economy. Fourth, public participation enhanced public control: if the state owned stock, and its men sat on the board, they could make sure the company acted in the public interest. Fifth, state investment might enrich the state. If the dreams of the enterprise came true, big dividends would flow to the public coffers. Pennsylvania, for example, not only owned stock in its banks, but after 1806, invested in turnpikes, bridge companies, canal companies and finally in railroads. States and cities both engaged in railroad boosting. Between 1827 and 1878, New York state lent, leased or donated $10,308,844.77 for construction of sixteen railroads. . . . Pennsylvania experimented with mixed public and private enterprises. At one stage in the state's marriage with its railroads, in the 1830's, Pennsylvania furnished locomotives; private companies supplied the other cars. Before 1842, the state of Maryland chose ten of the thirty directors of the Baltimore & Ohio; the city of Baltimore chose eight. In New Jersey, the "monopoly bill" of 1832 granted exclusive transport franchises in exchange for gifts of stock to the state.[5]

As late as 1838, conservative Daniel Webster held opponents of government economic intervention up to scorn: "Let the government attend to its own business and let the people attend to theirs. . . . These ominous sentences, Mr. President, have been ringing in my ears ever since they were uttered yesterday, by the Member from New York."[6] And Professor George Rogers Taylor, in his definitive *Economic History of the United States*, commented that during the early years of the Republic, Americans believed "that economic conditions should constantly improve and that government had a simple and direct obligation to take any practicable measure to forward such progress. Why should they fear the power of the state? Was it not their own creation in which the people themselves were sovereign?"[7]

This attitude did not last, of course. By the 1840s and 1850s, the public grew sour toward the ever-increasing number of corporations, their abuses and their bankruptcies. Then, after the Civil War, business leaders—firmly in the national saddle—themselves came to see less and less utility in state involvement. There was dual and converging disenchantment. By 1874, sixteen state constitutions refused to let the state own stocks in a corporation. In twenty states, the government had no power to lend its credit to any corporation. The federal government made its last land grant to railroads in 1872, and nearly all the new state constitutions of the 1870s forbade further local aid. Overall, the era in which the United States approached closest to laissez-faire was beginning, and although corporate America dominated our politics for a half-century after the 1870s, that control was used to minimize governmental involvement in the economy rather than to reestablish early-nineteenth-century business-government partnership. Since then, however, conservatives have to a large extent remained creatures of the laissez-faire psychology, fighting the extension of the public sector with antigovernment themes and rhetoric. That tradition has become increasingly less relevant in these days of growing global economic interdependence, in no small part because of the very different behavior of conservatives in Japan, France, Germany and other European countries.

THE INTERVENTIONIST TRADITION OF
CONSERVATISM

Unlike their American cousins, contemporary European conservatives draw on activist economic and philosophic traditions. State
intervention in the economy, taken for granted, has long been used
to advance national enterprise. And in the last few decades, conservative regimes in Europe, South America and East Asia have often
been in the vanguard of adopting state economic intervention mechanisms and national industrial policies.

A brief capsule account of what has gone on in these countries is
in order. I'll skim over the mechanics of economic policy and attendant organizational needs and emphasize the politics supporting both.
With the substantial, but not full, exception of Margaret Thatcher's
government, interventionist industrial policies in nations like Japan,
Germany and France—to say nothing of the approaches used by
Third World commercial contenders like Brazil and Korea—have
either been developed by or maintained under conservative governments. Economic activism amounts to a political and cultural consensus.

As for Germany and Japan, governments in both these countries
have long had a role in promoting players in their economics, being
directly responsible for industrialization in the late 1800s and early
1900s. Elite economic bureaucracies were created under Japan's
Meiji restoration and Bismarck's German unification policies. It's
fair to say that state guidance of the economy, accompanied by
nationalist assumptions, is virtually part of governmental culture in
these countries. Today's industrial policy apparatus—encompassing,
for example, Japan's Ministry of International Trade and Industry
and Germany's Ministry of Research and Technology, as well as the
Japan Development Bank and the German Development Bank—
requires little elaboration. Thus, even though Japan and Germany
are easing conspicuous government involvement in industrial planning, the political and economic tradition of the two countries is such
that the de facto government role remains important. And although
U.S. conservatives occasionally cite the market-oriented, supply-side
economic "miracle" of German Chancellor Ludwig Erhard or com-
mend recent reductions in Japanese tax rates, the basic political
economics of the two countries tilt local "conservatism" toward a
degree, if not a type, of government involvement more compatible

with Edward Kennedy than with Ronald Reagan.

Much the same circumstances prevail in France, where traditions of state economic involvement, reaching back to the militant mercantilism of Louis XIV, grew even more intense in Napoleon's time. In 1965, France became the first European country to introduce a scheme of cooperation between government and business on research and development projects. Positive steps to promote French industrial competitiveness in world markets and to increase France's energy independence were massively increased under the conservative government of Giscard d'Estaing, and by the 1970s, "no other European country had such a broad and explicit program of industrial policies" as did France.[8] Since 1975, French authorities have created three new funds to respond to growing structural problems in their economy: CIASI (1975), designed to rescue small and medium-sized companies; CIDISE (1978), to aid growing businesses with special easy loans; and FSAI (1978), a temporary mechanism to move northern and eastern French industry away from reliance on steel and coal.* One recent study of European industrial policies suggested that "France's decision in 1978 to provide grants and incentives to three electronics firms, each of which had taken a United States joint venture partner, and then to support success with purchase orders and additional funding, looked like a carbon copy of the Japanese practice of promoting high technology sectors in the manner of a horse breeder."[9] The point for U.S. conservatives is this: all of these ventures were launched under the aegis of the right-of-center regimes of de Gaulle and Giscard D'Estaing.†

The British case is rather different. During the Depression years,

---

*Comité Interministériel pour l'Aménagement des Structures Industrielles (CIASI) was replaced by Comité Interministériel de Restructuration Industrielle (CIRI). CIDISE is the acronym for Comité Interministériel pour le Développement des Investisements et le Soutien de l'Emploi. Fonds Speciales d'Adaptation Industrielle (FSAI) may no longer exist.

†Even Gaullist party leader Jacques Chirac, the present leader of French conservatism and a man otherwise inclined to liken himself to Ronald Reagan, comes down on the side of probusiness government involvement and activism. His chief deputy, Alain Juppe, says that planning under Chirac "would be more MITI than Gosplan" —that is, more Japanese than Soviet. Chirac himself, while pledging to denationalize a number of major industries—banks, automobiles and others—upholds planning: "The Socialists want to plan everything, including what we eat for breakfast. But a good planning system simply identifies four or five national objectives. These should be discussed with all segments of society" (*Wall Street Journal*, July 1, 1983).

the coalition Conservative government that took power in 1931 moved away from free-market economics toward trade protection and increased intervention in the economy. Later, in the early 1960s, when postwar industrial recovery lagged in some sectors, the Conservative party regime in power moved to create a National Economic Development Council (NEDC) and twenty-one economic development councils for specific industries. Designed to include representatives from management, labor and government, the councils were to serve an information and advisory function. They still exist, although other industrial policy mechanisms put in place by subsequent Labour party governments have been scrapped or curtailed by Conservative party regimes. Margaret Thatcher has been especially committed to reducing selective economic intervention and subsidies to state-owned industries in favor of reliance on macroeconomic policies for creating a more favorable environment for business expansion and investment. Even Mrs. Thatcher, however, upon her June 1983 election triumph, moved in several directions toward more government activity. Almost immediately, the previously separate ministries of trade and industry were combined to form a Ministry of Trade and Industry. Then, in July, the government announced a program under which employees will be able to keep current on the latest technologies affecting their work via home-learning packages offered by various colleges and industrial training groups under the aegis of the Department of Employment. The department is charged with ensuring that the courses offered are relevant to the strategically important sectors of British industry.[10] To a considerable extent, though, Britain remains the exception that proves the rule.

As in much of Western Europe and Japan, the rising economic powers of Asia and Latin America are also essentially neomercantilist. Two archetypal fast-growing nations run by right-wing strongmen, Korea and Brazil, both follow industrial policies and protectionist approaches to safeguarding domestic markets.

The ideological and economic bottom line is this: the United States is being pulled into a global economy in which it's no longer Caterpillar International Harvester but Caterpillar versus Komatsu and a supportive Tokyo government, in which it's no longer Boeing versus McDonnell-Douglas but Boeing versus Airbus and helpful European governments, and so on. American businessmen are no longer playing in a game governed by American rules. All of which brings us to the big question: will U.S. and British conservatives succeed as they try to restore the old marketplace verities that prevailed in the halcyon days of British and American economic dominion? Or will the approach subscribed to by the Japanese, Germans, French, Brazilians, Swedes, Koreans, Mexicans and all the rest win out? I, for one, am hard put to see how Britain and the United States now have the clout to rule the world political economy. And while Anglo-American commercial and ideological nostalgia can be a great vote-getter in Bournemouth or San Diego, it's not likely to influence policy makers in Paris, Bonn, Tokyo or Brasilia. Sooner or later, conservatives here are going to have to adapt to the new world political economy—and the sooner the better.

TRANSFORMATION OF CONSERVATIVE IDEOLOGY

So it is possible that U.S. conservatives are on the verge of an unenthusiastic philosophical transformation, and that they may out of necessity reacquaint themselves with government activism. Six circumstances point in that direction: first, because the globalization of the U.S. economy is forcing U.S. policy makers to start thinking in terms of policies and ideologies on an international and not just national basis; second, because Americans are slowly but steadily surrendering old ideas of U.S. uniqueness and beginning to borrow policy ideas and institutional approaches from abroad; third, because foreign business-government industrial partnerships are coming into our market, provoking businessmen and conservatives to enlist selective U.S. government economic intervention justified on nationalist grounds, thereby setting up a new ideological force; fourth, because new-wave technologies and modes of production—in this case, the microcircuitry of the information society—are especially likely to require some government nurturing in research and development, and in financial terms; fifth, because government must play a political role in developing a new telecommunications infrastructure, just as it did in developing the early industrial age's canals, turnpikes, telegraphs and railroads a century and a half ago; and sixth, because the "conservative" constituency is changing—becoming more populist. On all six counts, pragmatic conservatives are already moving toward a greater willingness to use government.

Globalization

The economy has become global, now that businessmen and workers in Pocatello, Idaho, and Erie, Pennsylvania, must go head to head with foreign competition for markets in Connecticut or Calcutta. As we face trade rivals aided by foreign governments, probusiness politicians develop a new perspective. Polling data cited on pages 79 and 91 illustrate that Americans already realize that, because of the role of foreign governments in their countries' economies, U.S. trade policy and domestic economic policy must be coordinated for the United States to keep pace. Conservatives are no less aware of the need for such a course than anyone else—and are just as much in agreement with this trend.

Borrowing Ideas from Abroad

It is apparent that Americans have lost much of their sense of national uniqueness and isolation. Much of that sense was shaped by the settlement patterns here—by the role of the frontier, by the sensibilities of immigrants rejecting Europe for somewhere new. Much of the American psychology, however, also had its origins in physical geography—namely, the extent to which the United States was isolated by two broad oceans while remaining self-sufficient behind tariff walls. Until the 1970s, imports and exports were only a minor blip on the U.S. economic oscilloscope. The result was that Americans were free to develop economic and political ideologies and institutions with very little sense of interaction with other nations. If it was part of the American frontier experience to reject or minimize government, there was little political or economic pressure from abroad to make us rethink that position. Except, of course, in wartime. And until the 1970s.

Now, by contrast, there's a growing sense among national opinion molders that we might do well to monitor and even imitate institutions and policy approaches practiced abroad. One can cite interest in: (1) a value-added (consumption-based) tax widely used in Europe; (2) some modification of the separation of powers between the executive and legislative branches to facilitate more effective economic policy making; (3) global, not domestic, measures of what should be unacceptable concentration under our antitrust laws; (4) increased business-government collaboration and labor-management cooperation, in the foreign manner; (5) some form of national industrial strategy; and (6) a U.S. version of the combined ministries of trade and industry found in many European and Far Eastern nations. If U.S. policy makers continue to move toward this package of ideas, political and economic ideology in the United States will undergo a major change, and rather quickly.

Growing Economic Nationalism as a Means to Activism

Let no one underestimate the growing strength of U.S. economic nationalism. Americans are not, by nature, especially eager to expand the role of government in any kind of way. Something has to push them, something has to stir up a set of feelings and attitudes that government must then serve and implement. In the early days of the republic, it was nationalism—westward expansion, the doctrine of Manifest Destiny and the like. In the first era of business nationalism, the United States as an independent nation was only a few decades old. Boundary disputes with Britain continued, and Spain was an untrusted neighbor to the south. Some of the best-known conservative public officials advocated building ships, subsidizing fisheries, protecting infant manufacturing industries from European competition, knitting the new country together and facilitating its industrial development with turnpikes, canals and railroads. As noted earlier, these conservatives called themselves Federalists, National Republicans and ultimately Whig Nationalists —among them were Alexander Hamilton, Henry Clay and Daniel Webster.

Some parallel circumstances exist today. In the 1980s—instead of Britain making moves on the Great Lakes, Spain plotting to the south, and infant industries being in danger—both our old, mature industries and our newly developed industries are similarly endangered. Japan has attacked the Great Lakes—or so Detroit would argue. Accordingly, economic nationalism and economic activism could easily gather momentum. And, just as the government role in the economy has always grown with war, so is it likely to grow with a sense of escalating economic competition.

Government Support for New Technology

As the information age begins, our economy has a group of new high-tech "infant" industries—such as fiber optics, microchips, robotics and biogenetics—that lay down a classic case for government assistance. In his "Report on the Subject of Manufactures," Alexander Hamilton argued that

> The continuation of bounties on manufactures long established must always be of questionable policy; because a presumption would arise, in every such case, that there were natural and inherent impediments to success. But, in new undertakings, they are as justifiable as they are oftentimes necessary. . . . There is no purpose to which public money can be more beneficially applied than to the acquisition of a new and useful branch of industry.[11]

In regard to precedents, bear in mind that commercial nationalism flourished during both great global economic watersheds: in the Renaissance, Reformation and rise of capitalism during the sixteenth century, and in the industrial revolution. Right now, the United States, Japan and Western Europe are competing to nurture high-tech growth industries the way England, Holland and Portugal competed for the East Indies spice trade four hundred years ago. Noninterventionist economics loses much of its relevance in this context. Meanwhile, at the local level, spirited competition among the various states of the Union to attract new technology is creating a situation in which local politicians call for government sponsorship of technological innovation commissions, of product development corporations and economic planning mechanisms even while they argue that no such federal agencies should be established in Washington.

Joint Development of a New Telecommunications Infrastructure

Although the press is full of articles about the decline of the old U.S. transportation and communications infrastructure—highways, bridges, railroads, mass transit—one can see only the bare beginnings of speculation about developing a new infrastructure: telecommunications. Historically, cities and towns have grown along major transportation routes, such as rivers, railroads and highway crossings, but the next "crossroads" could well be those places with access to modern electronic communications. Recently, three New York officials predicted that "a city's telecommunications infrastructure will be as critical an influence in business location and expansion decisions as its roads and water treatment capacity have been in the past."[12]

Perhaps. And perhaps not. But already debate has begun over the extent of the role government must play, and several major projects now under way, like the Teleport project to provide the New York metropolitan area with satellite communications, are business-government partnerships. Teleport is the joint effort of the Port Authority of New York and New Jersey, Merrill Lynch and Western Union. Such collaboration is analogous to investments made by New York and New Jersey in turnpikes, canals and railroads in an earlier era.

The Changing Conservative Constituency

Finally, I think we will see conservative economic policy change because the "conservative" constituency is changing. As I noted in my book *Post-Conservative America*, our "conservatism" no longer represents an elite group. To an increasing extent, the geographic home of the political right is the South and the West, once regions of populist and interventionist economics and areas nurtured by Washington with everything from naval training centers to aerospace contracts and cotton subsidies. The New Right electorates of the growing Sun Belt seem especially logical recruits for an activist economic nationalism.

For all these reasons, the context of economic policy making in the United States is changing in a way that must pull conservative politicians and theorists toward positions now held mainly by the more government-collaboration–minded elements of the corporate community. Or, to put things differently, one can see a change in the underlying economic basis of U.S. politics that is not yet mirrored in politics and ideology. But the change in politics and ideology will come as well.

There should be more than a little accompanying ideological upheaval because, in a larger sense, neither conservative nor liberal ideology seems especially suited to the new global challenge. If liberals are used to advocating state involvement in the economy, much of what they have advocated in the past is obsolete—even nostalgic—in both its form and its interest-group bias. Nor will it be easy to woo conservatives away from their absolute commitment to the old free-market system. Not to belabor terminology, but bear in mind that the developmental nationalism of the Hamiltonian era was *pre*conservative to the extent that Hamilton himself never used the label "conservative"; at his death in 1804, the term was just beginning to come into use in Europe. The reality is that both of our present ideological labels—conservative and liberal—are derived from the economic and political revolutionary ferment of the early nineteenth century, and may not be around much longer. In any case, postindustrial politics of the center-right must be increasingly activist. So "conservatives" are already finding themselves faced with an old challenge: adapt or die. With so much of the business community pointing in the right direction, I think they will adapt, though some ideological stalwarts will probably find the metamorphosis impossible.

CHAPTER

6

The Political Economics
of the 1980s

To date, the political response of the business and conservative communities has not matched their programmatic opportunity. Most participants in the national industrial strategy debate have been liberal. Yet the ambitions of those propounding a full-fledged interventionism exceed any plausible political consensus in the real world. Party divisions, to cite one factor, are such that Democrats will have trouble going beyond the stage of rhetoric. If they have most of the debaters, they also have most of the internecine warfare: labor versus high tech, Keynesian economists squabbling with structuralists, sunrise industry futurism versus sunset industry existing employment and clout.

That's why a bipartisan consensus set of constituencies should come to dominate. As conservatives grapple with the competitiveness issue, national trade and industrial strategy is likely to move away from left-liberal proposals on three dimensions: (1) toward a more articulated nationalism, (2) toward an increasing ideological moderation, with reliance where possible on market forces, and (3) toward a probusiness bias, though with business-labor collaboration. The irony is palpable. Just as it took Richard Nixon, a conservative of impeccable anti-Communist antecedents, to open up U.S. relations with the People's Republic of China in 1972, so conservative participation and support—although obviously they will not be labeled as such—may be necessary to put across the useful aspects of a national industrial policy. Massachusetts Senator Paul Tsongas, one of the better politicians in the so-called Atari Democrat camp, observed in a wry piece for the New York *Times* how easily Ronald Reagan could make some of these ideas his own. Should that happen, the senator urged Reagan, when signing the legislation into law, to "look over at us and wink so we will know that you know what we did."[1] To co-opt is the obvious strategy—in Disraeli's approximate words, to catch the Whigs bathing and steal their clothes (or at least the ones without holes).

THE FOUR MAJOR POLITICAL-ECONOMIC GROUPINGS

At some risk of oversimplification, the shape of U.S. economic strategy in the near future will be determined by the interaction of four principal groups: high-tech progressives (neoliberals), traditional liberal interventionists, free-market conservatives and pragmatic business moderate conservatives. Other elements, like the left and the New Right, are not very important here. My estimate is that the mid-decade center of gravity on industrial strategy issues lies with the business community's pragmatic conservatives. But let's look at all the aspirants.

Utopian High-Tech Progressives

High-tech progressives, or so-called Atari Democrats, have gotten a lot of scrutiny over the last few years. By early 1983, they were the height of fashion, although public and press enthusiasm has since cooled. Politically, there's less to them than meets the eye. Most Ataripols are upper-middle-class politicians, educated at Ivy League colleges, representing affluent districts with a substantial high-tech presence—among them are Senator Tsongas of Massachusetts, Senator Bill Bradley of New Jersey, Congressman Timothy Wirth of Colorado and Senator Gary Hart of Colorado. Talented as most of them are individually, theirs is not a constituency with great clout at the polls. Until he failed to win election to the U.S. Senate in 1982, California Governor Jerry Brown had also been a leading figure, heavily influenced and backed by high-tech executives like Intel Vice-Chairman Robert Noyce, Apple Computer founder Steve Jobs and Foothill Group Chairman Don Gevirtz.[2] As for their attendant thinkers, high-tech futurists like John Naisbitt sell books to a not dissimilar middle- and upper-middle-class constituency. Meanwhile, Harvard's Robert Reich and MIT's Lester Thurow are partially allied theorists.

I've been surprised how few observers have thought about how self-interested, electorally and economically, high-tech progressivism is. Abstract theorizing it is not, and there is a close match between its programs and its constituency. Of course, Ataripols would be for "growth instead of income redistribution," because they represent an important slice of affluent America. No Huey Long supporters in that crowd. Successful promotion of increased federal spending for education and research and development brings home the bacon for high-tech electorates just as navy contracts do in Charleston, South Carolina. The pork barrel is giving way to the quiche tray. Moreover, neoliberal legislators' free-trade biases are supported by the orientation of their state economies. Most come from the Northeastern and Pacific coast states—as well as from kindred areas like metropolitan Minneapolis, Tucson and Denver— boasting the nation's major concentrations of export-oriented and usually high-value-added manufactures. Small wonder that part of their economic rhetoric is devoted to reassuring what is essentially an upper-middle-class constituency that its future is secure. In 1983, Colorado Congressman Wirth said to *Business Week* that "what we're really trying to tell business is that we can be trusted."[3] By high-value-added business, at least. Certainly not by steel or textiles.

Like other spokesmen for emerging constituencies, Ataripols often become excessively enthusiastic. As they talk about an imminent new world of robots, lasers and megachips, high-tech advocates come across as a bit utopian, which is not surprising. Supporters of new economic frontiers tend to do that. Similar feelings were stirred up during the sixteenth-century overlap of the Renaissance, Reformation and rise of capitalism, as well as in the early-nineteenth-century industrial revolution. After all, Sir Thomas More wrote *Utopia* in 1516, amid the optimism of the Renaissance and commercial expansion. And three centuries later, in the industrial revolution, thinkers and poets like Ralph Waldo Emerson were mesmerized by the potential of the new economic mode. "Machinery and transcendentalism agree well," Emerson wrote, "stagecoach and railroad are bursting the old legislation like green withes. . . . Our civilization and these ideas are reducing the earth to a brain. . . . See how by telegraph and steam the earth is anthropologized."[4] In England, poet laureate Alfred Lord Tennyson got equally carried away in his nineteenth-century verse.

Appropriately enough, similar "Chipward, Ho!" optimism has left high-tech progressives with a credibility problem among older Democratic constituencies, especially labor and racial minorities, two groups the Ataripol approach of government favoritism to high tech would leave behind. The more pragmatic high-tech politicians, attuned to compromise, wisely try to mute the implications. Some high-tech thinkers have less reticence. John Naisbitt dismisses unions as "dinosaurs," suggesting that we are en route not only to becoming an information society but to becoming an almost union-free society.[5] Lester Thurow favors implementing an explicit industrial policy to favor high-tech, high-value-added industries while encouraging "disinvestment" in older industries: "Instead of adopting public policies to speed up the process of disinvestment, [the government] acts to slow it down with protection and subsidies for the inefficient. If we cannot learn to disinvest, we cannot compete in the growth race."[6] All of which has led Sheldon Friedman, research director for the United Auto Workers, to charge that neoliberalism is "very deterministic stuff. It says, 'Once you've lost it, you've lost it, and it's not even worth trying to save.' You're writing off an awful lot of workers, and that's very undemocratic."[7] Robert Kuttner, editor of *Working Papers*, sees labor as the neoliberal Achilles heel: "If you switch from steel to semiconductors, you go from union to non-union and I don't see how you can get [AFL-CIO President] Lane Kirkland to sign onto that bargain."[8] And Brian Turner, director of legislation and economic policy for the AFL-CIO, says: "It's condescending for these guys to say we ought to just walk away from autos and steel work. What happens to the 10 million to 15 million people whose livelihood depends on them? High tech doesn't have an answer. All these people can't leap from that abandoned industrial base onto this little tiny silicon chip for our future. There's not enough room."[9]

Rhode Island economic consultant Ira Magaziner, a national industrial policy advocate sympathetic to basic industry, told a Great Lakes governors' conference in 1983 that "if all the high-tech activities increased one hundred percent every year for several years—which they will not—you still would not have a fifth of the jobs that you have in autos and steel."[10] One recent analysis quoted an executive of Digital Equipment saying, "It's just wrong to hold out hope for high tech as a mass producer of jobs. Increasingly, it's an elite industry for individuals."[11] In a July 1983 article for the Washington *Post*, Gerald W. McEntee, president of the American Federation of State, County and Municipal Employees, posed the question "Is high tech unpatriotic?"—because of its use of tax breaks to "ship jobs overseas."[12] And MIT Professor William E. Griffith told an international conference: "The more high tech triumphs, the more it will increase social stratification, most of all, unfortunately, in the United States. Like the industrial revolution, it will, left to its own devices, mercilessly close outmoded, inefficient industries and leave their workers unemployed."[13] Analyses like these point out the limitations of high-tech politics within the Democratic party.

Part of the disarray among Democrats reflects fear that high tech could eliminate quite a number of existing low- and middle-level white-collar jobs. Employment statistics show word processors swallowing secretarial jobs, desk-top computers replacing clerks, and automatic banking machines replacing tellers. There's even a racial problem. A Boston *Globe* survey of black employment in Massachusetts high-tech industries found it running well below black employment in industries offering work at comparable organizational levels—clerical, professional, technical or whatever—in the overall metropolitan Boston labor market.[14] Accordingly, minorities are unlikely to show much sympathy for high-tech dreams and aspirations.

As for constituencies, the conflict between Atari and blue-collar Democrats pivots on the party's fundamental schism, which has been widening since the 1960s. On one side are middle- and upper-middle-income postindustrial voters who are socially progressive but affluent enough to want to be conservative in their economics. On the other side is the older, larger, economically redundant Democratic constituency of rural and small-town Southerners and Northern blue-collar workers, and, in this case, also minorities. The split is easy to paper over, but not to resolve. Dissension over industrial policy is just the newest gap along an important socioeconomic fault line. For Ataripols, the political and economic problems are essentially that the future is not coming as quickly—or as cleanly—as they would like.

Traditional Liberal Interventionists

If Atari Democrats are a putative Third Wave constituency, the old Democratic constituencies are usually Second Wave or earlier: the technologically obsolete and, in some cases, the technologically hopeless, to use sociologist David Apter's phrase. At the extremes, that phrase fits. So does Robert Reich's caricature of political-economic "historic preservation." Senator Edward Kennedy has gone so far as to call for full resurrection of the steel industry, and some of the greatest applause for Walter Mondale has followed calls for trade protection measures.

National public opinion supports protectionism, of course. Increased tariffs, import restrictions and domestic content legislation all won support—and lopsidedly—in surveys made in 1982 and 1983. This, to some extent, is a manifestation of frustration vying with nostalgia. If the American public could, by snapping its fingers, restore the steel, auto, rubber and glass industries to the condition they were in during the halcyon days of the 1950s, it certainly would. Let us admit that. And if the public thought that a second round of the New Deal—another Reconstruction Finance Corporation, another National Recovery Act, another Work Projects Administration, another Civilian Conservation Corps—would score a second success, it would embrace that, too.

Fortunately, the evidence suggests that most Americans don't think it's possible to return to the 1930s—or to the 1950s. They know we've got a very different economy now and face very different prospects. But if the high-tech neoliberals are trying to hurry history up, the old-line Democratic preservationist-protectionist elements are trying to slow it down—or even recapture the economic past. The public knows better, and similar comprehension can be found in Britain, Canada and Western Europe as well. People understand that many of the jobs lost in heavy industries during the past five years will never be recovered, and that to try to recover them would be foolish.

To a partial extent, though, traditional liberal economic interventionists may enjoy another period in the sun during the 1980s. Excessive as their remedies may be, tied to fading interest groups as they may be, interventionists do have their finger on both a national sentiment and a national need when they call for a business-government partnership, for rebuilding America's transportation infra-

structure, for developing a new model of management-labor relations, and for using a tough trade posture as a lever to force new,
fairer global trading rules. This ideology has a role to play. During
the late 1970s and early 1980s, free-market economics was ascendant
and usefully grappled with a number of problems widely ignored by
liberals—from tax reduction to overregulation. Laissez-faire left the
problems of the global marketplace virtually untouched, however,
and careful intervention is part of the remedy.

Nevertheless, beyond the revalidation of Rooseveltian esprit, several of the programmatic specifics put forward by the neo–New
Dealers go too far, especially the call for a government agency to
restructure our heavy industry or to pick industry-by-industry winners and losers. As for protectionist trade proposals—domestic content laws, higher tariffs or a major indulgence in import quotas—
these can be justified as a bargaining tool, but no more. That is
yesterday's stuff; affirmative attempts to reshape global trade rules
are today's.

Both the high-tech neoliberals and the neo–New Dealers have a
vision of America, be it as it was in the past or as it will be in the
future. Each has an appeal accordingly. Their *compromise* agendas,
however—the stuff hammered out by liberal think tanks, party task
forces and congressional Democratic caucuses—tend to be a catalog
of mutually acceptable half-measures that lack the clear constituency
appeal of either side. What the Democrats do have, though, and what
conservatives will have to borrow from them in order to succeed
themselves, is their fundamental awareness—a legacy handed down
from Andrew Jackson through Franklin D. Roosevelt, Harry Truman and John Kennedy—that government intervention is often necessary to mobilize an economy in crisis. If anything, the need for that
approach is very great today, given foreign business-government
collaboration.

Free-Market Conservatives and Nationalism

Free-market conservatives entered 1984 with a mixed record. If the
Reagan innovative market-based economic policies had been a total
failure, Washington would now be battening down the hatches for
a fling at an ill-considered, excessively interventionist national industrial policy. Not so, of course. Reagan policies did fall far short
of promises made by ardent supply-side, deregulationist and

monetarist advocates early in the game. Perfection was not achieved, and our economy could not be—and was not—transformed and righted simply by cutting taxes, by rolling back economic regulation, by shrinking the money supply and by trying to reduce the public sector's share of the Gross National Product. On the other hand, the economy recovered enough—especially after the Reagan fiscal and monetary course was changed in mid-1982—to be able to profit from some of the tax-cut, disinflation and deregulation efforts launched earlier, and this recovery has worked to create a more balanced perception of our true status. On the one hand, economic policy from 1981 to 1983 did break enough of the promises originally made by its advocates—who were unable, among other things, to deliver the country from a severe global recession—so that the public now again supports a new round of limited government economic intervention and involvement. At the same time, however, Reagan's economic policy succeeded in enough ways so as to convince the public that a return to traditional liberalism would be unwise and unjustified, and to give the conservative center-right political camp an effective veto over anything but a moderate national economic and trade strategy.

This is not to say that free-market theorists have warmed to the concept of a compromise approach. Very few have. In fact, most of them see any move along these lines as implying a repudiation of the early Reagan ideological experiment. There's some truth in that, but they're being too touchy. In the spring of 1983, for example, supply-side economist Bruce Bartlett, executive director of the Congressional Joint Economic Committee, leaped to the ideological barricades. In an analysis for the *Wall Street Journal* he predicted that "the key economic issue of the 1984 elections, regardless of who the candidates are, will be the establishment of a national industrial policy for the United States"—and then went on to deplore the idea as a device for Democrats to make inroads into the business community.[15] He saw a Machiavellian scheme afoot. Via a national industrial policy, Democrats would get a chance to "implement policies which would have the effect of taxing Republican areas of the country in order to shore up the economies of Democratic states," notably the steel, auto and textile states "largely represented by Democrats." In fact, this last assertion will be news to the two Republican senators from the steel state of Pennsylvania, Arlen Specter and H. John Heinz III, and to the Republican parties of the textile states of Virginia and the

Carolinas, which in 1984 sent one Democrat and five Republicans to the United States Senate. And it will also surprise the conservative executives of the industries involved.

By contrast, it is essential to consider the words of respected center-right free-marketeers like former Council of Economic Advisers Chairmen Herbert Stein and Murray Weidenbaum in order to strike a serious national balance. Both men—and others too numerous to mention—have disdained federal industrial agency proposals as counterproductive government intervention in the economy. And as these and related arguments take hold, the competitiveness debate is tilting toward the business agenda. My own sense is that a business-oriented competitiveness agenda provides *reinforcement* for balanced conservative politics, not vitiation.

Changing global circumstances have provided the incentive. Public demand is increasing for two things: a more assertive world-wide protection of U.S. economic interests and a spur to government for it to "do something." In this regard, both conservatives and liberals have reasons to be wary. Conservatives distrust government economic intervention; liberals distrust nationalism.

One can argue that, in the real world, conservatives will be pulled toward interventionism by nationalism, while liberals will be pulled toward nationalism by interventionism. But although there's evidence that both things are happening, nationalism seems to be the more critical emerging force. For example, a poll by the Los Angeles *Times* in May 1983 identified economic fear of Japan as a dominant component of U.S. sentiment.

Attitudes towards Japan contribute significantly to Americans' opinions about foreign trade in general. Protectionism received strong support by a very wide 80% to 16% margin among the relatively small group who showed an anti-Japanese sentiment in response to such questions as which nation they viewed least favorably or whether they still get angry when they think about Pearl Harbor.

Many Americans continue to blame Japanese competition for the nation's economic problems, along with foreign oil prices and Congress. When given the ability to choose several options, about 48% consider foreign oil prices very much or almost completely to blame for current economic conditions, while 43% single out Congress and 41% blame the Japanese.

Similarly, 56% of all Americans think import competition from Japan does more harm than good to the United States and 42% of the public believes there should be less trade with Japan, while only 15% think there should be more.[16]

Somewhat parallel data had also emerged in early 1982 surveys—one taken by Potomac Associates and Gallup for NHK Japanese television, the second by Louis Harris for the *Asahi Shimbun* newspaper. The Potomac Associates/NHK television poll found that between 1980 and 1982, favorable attitudes toward the Japanese had dropped from 84 percent to 63 percent.[17] More importantly, opinion polls suggest increasing public awareness that foreign governments in general, and not just Japan's, are working to aggrandize their own exports, in the process undercutting the international economic position of the United States.

All these forces and factors have combined to increase American popular frustration. In consequence, opinion data and business organization proposals alike mirror an increasingly nationalist attitude toward U.S. trade policy. Conservative ideology is not simply a matter of economics. Especially since the mid-1960s—and since the Sun Belt substantially transformed U.S. conservatism into an anti-Establishment, flag-waving credo—nationalist themes have been important to center-right politicians. Under the circumstances, and assuming that fierce global economic competition will continue, it's likely that nationalism will outweigh adherence to strict free-market ideology among much of the conservative electorate.*

Big-Business Moderate Conservatism as a Center of Gravity

Scratch a big-business executive, and you'll find someone almost as suspicious of public opinion as he is of media bias. Populism and nationalism call up few toasts at annual meetings of the Business Council. To the extent that major U.S. corporations have found themselves affected in the past by the currents of popular national-

---

*For example, in mid-1983, five New Right leaders, led by *Conservative Digest* publisher Richard Viguerie, issued a joint statement criticizing the recent special meeting in Geneva on the General Agreement on Tariffs and Trade (GATT) as an example of the one-way protectionist attitude of most other nations: "All of these countries want their own products—many of which they directly subsidize—to be sold in the U.S. without any restraints whatsoever. But these same nations have conjured up all kinds of tariffs, import quotas, local-content requirements, advertising restrictions, special regulations, and other trade barriers to limit the availability of imported products. It is absurd for us to allow ourselves to be taken advantage of so tremendously. It amounts to economic unilateral disarmament."

ism, the impact has usually been negative. Remember, by way of historical example, popular charges that the United States was dragged into World War I by munitions makers or to safeguard the loans of Wall Street banks. Out in the lonely rural precincts of bellwether isolationism, the upper reaches of corporate and financial America have traditionally been suspect of internationalism—most recently in the debate over the unpopular Panama Canal treaties, so enthusiastically promoted by the American banks with loans and operations in Panama. It's a bit of a turnabout, then, for so many of the country's major corporations and business organizations to have proposed the nationalist trade themes and agendas catalogued earlier. But they have. And the resulting political opportunity may be considerable. Nationalism—even trade and economic nationalism—plays in Peoria. One can plausibly expect Bethlehem Steel, du Pont and Westinghouse to elicit a lot more grass-roots support when they contend with Tokyo, Bonn and Paris than when they spar with Ralph Nader, the AFL-CIO or the Justice Department.

And thus the extraordinary new politics: the developing corporate agenda for stricter trade law enforcement, action against foreign industrial policies, and orchestrated remobilization of research and education adds up to a sober, sophisticated middle way between simplistic, door-slamming protectionism on the one hand and naïve free-trade sentiment on the other. It's assertive and nationalist enough for the public, yet antiprotectionist enough to draw grudging tolerance from free-traders. It also constitutes the middle ground between high-tech utopianism and historic preservation of basic industries, and between right-wing free-market adherence and leftist excessive economic interventionism.

The approach is also reasonably compatible with Republican trade policy. The Council of Economic Advisers, long a free-trade bastion, embraced critical elements of the business nationalist posture in its 1983 Report to Congress. In that document, the council asserted that "even though costly to the U.S. economy in the short run, [retaliation] may . . . be justified if it serves the strategic purpose of increasing the cost of [trade interventions] by foreign governments." And in early 1983, William Krist, President Reagan's Assistant U.S. Trade Representative for Industrial Policy, suggested:

There is a dilemma. It would appear that the United States cannot function as an industrial democracy with industrial policy or compete in world markets without an industrial policy. However, there is a middle route that seeks to preserve freedom and efficiency for U.S. consumers and producers and at the same time counters the deleterious impact of targeting policies embodied in the industrial policies of many countries. Such a middle course could consist of the following types of elements.

The first element would be to review major U.S. governmental policies to ensure they are not detrimental to the trade performance of U.S. industries. Because U.S. industries are by definition in the international arena, many major policy decisions can have implications for U.S. imports or exports. Formulation of new policies should include consideration of their impact on trade. Existing policies that are identified as having a negative trade impact or lacking a potentially beneficial impact should be systematically reviewed for reformulation.[18]

If the Reagan administration has been gravitating toward the business nationalist agenda, so has Republican and conservative rank-and-file opinion. Grass-roots free-trade fidelity seems exhausted. For example, an early 1983 national survey by Penn-Schoen (Garth Analysis) found Republicans roughly as supportive of trade protectionism as Democrats. Note the partisan breakdown of responses to the following extreme question: "Would you be *more* or *less* likely to support a candidate for President who was for high tariffs against the Japanese and other foreign products, in order to protect American industry and jobs?" Seventy percent of the Democrats and 61 percent of the Republicans said they'd be more likely to support a high tariff backer, while 19 percent of the Democrats and 24 percent of the Republicans said they would be less likely.[19] Tariffs, of course, are not a usable mechanism these days. But the point is that Republicans seem just as willing as the blue-collar Democratic rank-and-file to embrace a new tough attitude toward trade. There is little support for those who say that conservative or GOP electorates insist on rigid free-market adherence in global economics.

Table 10 represents persuasive evidence that free-market opponents of liberal industrial policy give substantial support to the milder interventionist ingredients of industrial strategy. Indeed, as the table shows, free-market supporters in the business community are almost as likely as industrial policy backers to endorse a wide array of competitiveness measures.

TABLE 10.
*Proposals Favored by Business Executives to Help
Improve U.S. Productivity and Global Competitiveness*

	Total Executives (%)	Market-Forces Executives (%)	Industrial Policy Executives (%)
Increased government spending:			
Incentives to retrain workers	76	72	80
Scientific and technological research	68	63	76
Science and engineering education	66	60	77
Loans and tax credits for ventures with strong export potential	55	50	64
Regulatory reform:			
Allow private joint-venture research	73	69	79
Allow tax write-offs for investment in small companies	68	68	69
Allow use of pension funds for high-tech venture capital	55	53	56
Newly created entities and procedures:			
National development corporation to help modernize basic industries	54	49	63
Labor-management negotiations, with federal incentives, to revitalize basic industries	54	49	62
Cabinet-level trade department	52	51	55
Cabinet-level science and technology department	49	45	57
Federal planning agency for long-term economic forecasting in advisory capacity	49	44	57

Note: Based on 523 interviews with top and mid-level executives (329 market-forces executives; 192 industrial policy executives) in Fortune 500 manufacturing firms and in the 50 largest companies in banking, utilities, transportation, merchandising, life insurance and diversified finance.

SOURCE: Adapted from Opinion Research Corporation, Executive Caravan Management Profile, Summer 1983.

The basic policy divisions were elicited from 523 executives during April-May 1983 by the Opinion Research Corporation:

"Regarding the development of our economy, which of these two statements comes closer to your own view?"

> The development of our national economy during the 1980s will work best if market forces are permitted to determine what direction business and industry should take and government plays a less interventionist role by removing some of the regulatory barriers   63%

> Because of dramatic structural changes in our economy and increased international competition, the U.S. needs to establish a coordinated long-range industrial policy, based on intensified cooperation among business, labor and government   37%

Republicans, moreover, are just as interventionist in their willingness to see the federal government help business meet foreign competition. A late 1982 Louis Harris/*Business Week* survey found GOP voters exceeding Democrats in support for the bulk of a hypothetical government agenda to help business become more competitive internationally. The majority of Republicans polled agreed with proposals to: "get labor and industry to swap lower wage increases for a more competitive economy—and more jobs"; "use windfall profits taxes on oil to help industries and provide seed money for high-tech companies"; and "give tax breaks and subsidies to companies that compete with foreign subsidized companies."[20] To the third proposal, by the way, Republicans gave considerably more backing than Democrats.

Thus business is in a rare—almost unique—position to serve as a rallying point for a coalition of interests and attitudes. One reason why the public appears willing to embrace a proindustrial strategy is that there's little sign that the nation agrees with the "management crisis" charge made by leading neoliberals—the argument that declining global competitiveness basically reflects the failing of American corporate management. Admittedly, Americans think our complacent, stodgy, short-term–oriented management has been a factor in the decline. But, generally speaking, surveys probing public views on responsibility for the plight of the economy reveal that blame is assigned equally to labor, management, government, Congress, Japan and OPEC. Of course, poor management was a factor. Yet so were high wages. So were heavy-handed government regulators. So were bumbling administrators and inept Congresses. What's more, the public hasn't registered any great faith in economists or journalists, either. Finally, it's important to keep in mind that the feeling is widespread in Britain and in the United States that the old industrial economies are in fundamental transition—a thesis made evident by the transition pains experienced in so many countries. Although U.S. leadership elites—in business, government, labor, academia and the media—haven't shown much sensitivity to the long term in the last decade, the public isn't blaming any one group for our problems. And that's the point, politically. The notion that corporate managers are solely responsible—that their undoubted "paper entrepreneurial-ism" was all cause and not substantially effect—is grossly exaggerated. It's a case of 1980s overstatement to match the overblown 1970s conservative rhetoric proclaiming that nothing was wrong with the economy that couldn't be cured by getting government regulators off the backs of hard-working businessmen.

In a related matter, one early 1983 survey, by pollsters Penn and Schoen for the Garth Analysis, asked Americans which factor they blamed for the declining competitiveness of U.S. goods, "high wages for American workers" or "inefficient American management"? Opinion split right down the middle—43 percent on each side. Which brings out another facet of the political economics of the 1980s. Partly because voters blame both management *and* labor for the decline of the economy, they do not appear disposed to condemn either side, instead preferring and hoping for a new spirit of labor-management cooperation. Here again, business moderate conserva-tism—the view taken by the companies in the Business Roundtable, the Committee for Economic Development and the Labor-Industry Coalition for International Trade—represents a cooperative "middle way" between labor's own past-oriented agenda and the disdain for labor's interests displayed by many high-tech futurists and free-market conservative ideologues. The basis for mutuality seems very real.

All in all, I cannot remember another time when a potential business agenda was so centrally placed to become the consensus and to dominate a vital national political debate.

THE POLITICS OF A COMPETITIVENESS COALITION

The bottom line politically is this: a new round of government involvement in the economy is developing, and the question is who is to control it. If conservatives abdicate and liberals win—which I don't think will happen—we could well see U.S. management practices made the scapegoat again. Opinion could possibly lurch toward a new array of government mechanisms—investment banks, redevelopment authorities and the like—to usurp private corporate managers' authority on behalf of politicians and government regulators. That becomes a clear possibility if the economy slips into another recession in 1985–86. On the other hand, if business and conservative strategists co-opt the trend and shape new government involvement toward a "support enterprise" direction, then the new agenda could have a conservative cutting edge.

National election years are always an occasion for bringing industrial growth or redevelopment ideas to the fore. Past presidential campaigns have nurtured protectionist appeals to key industrial regions—not least Richard Nixon's 1972 Southern strategy, which was linked to textile quotas. A competitiveness agenda and a presidential campaign could make for some dramatic politics.

As for constituencies, what can be called a new proindustrial assertiveness taps a political coalition reaching well beyond the Fortune 500 and related organizations. Large elements of organized labor would perceive policy movement as favorable to them, as would many high-tech companies. Even though free-market conservatives might be miffed in some ways, nationalist themes would rally many of them; if the Sun Belt is the most entrepreneurial, free-market–oriented region of the United States, it is also the most nationalistic.

The important and pivotal distinction to make is that the nationalism of the Sun Belt is aggressive, assertive and expansionist, not status quo—or *status quo ante*—protectionist. Pennsylvania and Michigan want to preserve and protect their declining industries' share of what has been a huge and prosperous domestic market. That's not enough for a persuasive politics for a national electorate. By contrast, Florida, Texas, Arizona and California want to break down foreign restraints, be they Japan's de facto exclusion of U.S. tobacco, official foreign subsidies or preferences to local high tech, growing overseas obstacles to U.S. banking and insurance, or the

European Community's subsidy and protection of local agriculture, among other barriers.

In a perceptive analysis for the Dallas *News*, Richard Fisher, former executive assistant to the Secretary of the Treasury and now resident manager in Dallas for the private investment banking firm of Brown Brothers Harriman & Company, suggested that the political economics of the Sun Belt was characterized by minimal organized labor influence; an aggressive approach to the world community, coupled with a lack of the Eastern Establishment's traditional ties to Europe; and a generally minimal concern for the workings of the international monetary system. To some extent, labor's low influence means a general tolerance of foreign heavy-industry competition. Then Fisher goes on to say:

> But this does not translate into a lack of support for protectionism. It simply means protectionist impulses are of a different form: they are offensive rather than defensive. They insist on the reciprocity of open markets elsewhere.
>
> One likely outcome of increased sensitivity by U.S. leaders to trade policy biases of the Southern/Western power base will be increased intolerance for the protectionist fabric of the EEC or any other markets and, indeed, demand for change.[21]

Clearly, the aggressive capitalists of the Sun Belt are not going to look favorably on the old-style protectionist approaches or the economic interventionism of the new New Dealers. Old-style protectionism would retard Sun Belt growth and the emergence of its power. What Sun Belt voters and interest groups are likely to support, however, includes basic industry demands for full enforcement of U.S. laws, trade reciprocity and action against foreign industrial policies, not least because of the growing shared concern of Sun Belt semiconductor and data-processing companies. That's where the overlap between the constituencies lies.

Equally important, any new U.S. trade and economic strategy in the 1980s will represent not so much a triumph of any one side as a fusion of ideas and viewpoints that tilt in the business nationalist direction. High-tech advocates will see a new national commitment to education and scientific research and development rivaling the mobilization that swept across the country after Sputnik. The new New Dealers will see some cherished notions of government intervention in the economy at least partially validated. Nationalists will see a new trade aggressiveness against the mercantilism of Europe and East Asia. Free-market advocates, for their part, have made a strong enough case recently to rebut proposals for restructuring industry under the benevolent aegis of Washington officials.

Readers of *National Review* on the right and *The Nation* on the left will dissent. Free-market purists will talk of 1930s economic corporatism and the return of Benito Mussolini. Libertarians will still want government to wither and disappear. High-tech futurists will think the economy is assuredly demassifying into something much better. And finally, leftists will continue to be ever fearful of a Pentagon–big-business axis.

If one wants to be pessimistic, there is some truth in many of these concerns. For me, public opinion began to move during the 1960s and 1970s toward a certain politics of middle-class frustration, including a desire for a kind of strong leadership able to mobilize national unity and purpose behind some cause. Middle-class populism of this sort —middle-class radicalism, really—can often be a prelude to corporatism. Nationalism and labor-management cooperation are recurrent and linked themes, too. Such a politics typically tries to submerge old divisions—of caste, class, labor and capital—through a new unity in the corporate state. Elements of that are evident again.

It's well to remember, however, that charges of Mussolini-style corporatism were made against Franklin D. Roosevelt and the New Deal during the 1930s. In fact, the reverse was true. The evidence is that the New Deal co-opted the corporatist impulse and the potential frustration of the middle class during the Depression. What could have gone out of control didn't. A new economic nationalism could play a similar role now. Popular fears and frustrations could be channeled into a crusade for a resurgence of a robust American economy.

Thus the political opportunity. Not to shape a new party majority —that probably won't happen when the parties themselves are disintegrating—but to build an important coalition for national revitalization.

CHAPTER
7

Monongahela Realpolitik: Politics, Interest Groups and a Workable National Industrial Strategy

Germany's "Iron Chancellor," Otto von Bismarck—a business nationalist if ever there was one—defined politics as "the doctrine of the possible, the attainable . . . the art of the next best."[1] His words are certainly important now. And because economic problems demand an attainable response, the most plausible remedies seem to be coming from businessmen, not academicians or ideologues.

There's little reason to assume ideology has an answer. A successful economic mobilization will involve the meshing of commonsense solutions—most of them not even very innovative—with demonstrated political and public preferences. Time, meanwhile, is of the essence, because of the worsening U.S. trade deficit, the plight of American basic industry and the real possibility of yet another economic downturn sometime soon. The public's eagerness to act is not much in doubt. The issue is whether our leadership will dilute the strong desire for protectionism by channeling it into more constructive avenues.

DEFINING THE POSSIBLE

Feasibility and consensus are imperative. Of the fifteen proposals set forth earlier, a dozen have come from business organizations. Most of them have broad-based interest-group support and in many cases relatively little dedicated interest-group opposition. What's more, in the right circumstances, the appeal of the programmatic whole—the general idea of mobilizing Americans around a theme of national economic renewal and global competitiveness—could exceed the appeal of the sum of the parts. Technical propositions can never be the stuff of national enthusiasms. A threatened decline in the standard of living, until now taken for granted, can be. In short, we'll show those Japanese (or Germans, or French) a thing or two.

The Politics of Government Intervention

No serious agenda for renewal can propose that government has the answers. Unless there is a new recession, any plausible trade and industrial strategy must not include a national central planning mechanism or a development agency empowered to make or break individual industries or companies. Improved national economic policy coordination is something else; the Reagan White House itself in 1983 proposed a Cabinet-level council to advise the President on the performance and competitive position of U.S. industry. The distinction between the two approaches, however—intervention versus coordination—is important, because of public and elite reluctance to embrace a new big role in the economy for Washington. In 1983, for instance, a Los Angeles *Times* survey revealed that 50 percent of those polled felt that the government should take a smaller role in business planning and allow normal competition to govern foreign trade, while only 38 percent of the respondents favored a larger government role in business planning to help U.S. companies compete more profitably. Unfortunate terminology—invocation of government involvement in actual "business planning"—may have influenced the results, but public skepticism of government interference is manifest.

As table II shows, there is considerable support for a new agency to help basic industry. There is much less backing, however, for the sort of broad industrial policy in which government agencies would determine industrial and technological priorities. Important as it is to maintain redundant Northern basic industries, the events of 1983 and 1984 show just how many Democrats harbor major reservations. Business-minded moderates are skeptical, of course. Several former Democratic federal budget directors and presidential economic advisers have rejected the idea of an industrial policy. By late 1983, most leading Atari Democrats had shifted to oppose the idea of a new Reconstruction Finance Corporation. Finally, of course, most economists have suggested that an industrial policy is unnecessary, citing the argument that much of the industrial predicament of 1981 through 1983 can be laid at the door of bad macroeconomic policy —high interest rates, erratic monetary policies, an inadequate tax code, excessive federal budget deficits.

TABLE II.

Opinion Leaders' View of Establishing a New Government Agency to Provide Loans to Basic Industry

	Favor (%)	Oppose (%)
Business executives	30	67
Union leaders	74	26
Elected government officials	56	43
Appointed government officials	56	38
Public interest group officials	53	44
Media representatives	43	53
Academicians	37	61
TOTAL OPINION LEADERS	45	53

SOURCE: Opinion Research Corporation poll, 1983.

The upshot is a rather clear indication that a national industrial strategy must concentrate on leveling the international playing field for U.S. service, high-tech and basic industries, and not on any grand new government schemes. For the mid-1980s, at least, a limited agenda is a logical agenda.

The Need for Prompt Action

The time to launch a national strategy was yesterday. Some analysts have projected that our trade deficit—the excess of imports over exports—could surpass $100 billion in 1984. Partly because of changing global economic patterns and partly because of the impact of the recently overvalued dollar, a number of export-oriented industries remain on the economic ropes, as the recovery has been one of the most uneven in memory.

But besides the need to support American exports to increasingly endangered markets, there's a second reason to get a moderate industrial strategy in place during 1984 and 1985. By late 1983, surveys of business and financial economists were turning up a high degree of concern that the recovery would slacken and slide into recession again by 1985 or 1986. Without a tougher U.S. trade posture in place by that time, the impact on marginal American industry, and thus on employment and on politics, would be substantial. Interventionist politicians would once again point to the lights going out in Midwestern steel furnaces and once again ask for a centralized industrial policy.

So the time to take a sound approach is now.

The Importance of Existing Business and Labor Interest Groups

Any plausible national industrial strategy—whether the fifteen proposals outlined earlier or any other—can and should harness the self-interest of a broad range of established industries and lobbies. Proposals that preach the distant splendors of high tech fail that test. So do narrow proposals to reconstitute New Deal institutions or to preserve the New Deal's New York City–Pittsburgh–Detroit electoral-economic axis. A successful political and legislative appeal to the requisite number of interest groups—business and labor alike—should lie in a program that moves in obvious, consensus-backed directions and deals with the generally recognized problems of existing basic and high-tech industries, especially those caused by unfair foreign practices.

This is not the same thing as agreeing to restore the *status quo ante* of a handful of redundant industries. At the same time, however, it does mean recognizing that existing economic interest groups have compiled a large list of valid complaints about economic and trade strategy—or the lack thereof. And the approach also recognizes that careful selection of reasonable complaints and sophisticated proposals to remedy them is a good premise on which to base a sound national strategy that is likely to be supported by voters. From this standpoint, the proindustrial "competitiveness agenda" approach is politically realistic, while that of the left is questionable.

Besides, up to a point, there's simply a good deal of merit in assisting economic sectors undercut by unfair foreign competition. Serious injury has been suffered all over. From data-processing firms on the high-tech corridor along Route 128 in Massachusetts to semiconductor firms in California's Silicon Valley, scores—probably hundreds—of American corporations on the technological cutting edge have called for a new aggressiveness against foreign industrial policies. Fortunately, implementation of this agenda would simultaneously provide some relief and breathing space for the embattled basic industries of the Great Lakes and Southeast. Moreover, if steel, auto and textile leaders can be drawn away from their current near-protectionism into a more strategic posture, the country as a whole will profit. And make no mistake about it, our nation does need to develop a sophisticated response to foreign industrial policies, and national leaders must divert the leverage of the Great Lakes and the Southeast from tariff- and domestic-content–type remedies into some other solutions.

No one should underplay the politics here. That's because the Great Lakes states—especially Pennsylvania, Ohio, Michigan, Illinois and Wisconsin—and the Southeast—Alabama, Georgia and the Carolinas—have become decisive battlegrounds of presidential election strategy. Pivotal electoral votes, in turn, mean circumstances in which politicians are willing to cater to troubled industries and protectionist psychologies. Richard Nixon's 1972 "Southern Strategy," as noted, included a quota system for the protection of Dixie's textile industry. Then in 1980, the concern of both incumbent Jimmy Carter and candidate Ronald Reagan for helping the steel and automobile industries seemed to reach full pitch between the spring primaries in Pennsylvania, Michigan and Ohio and the November general election. The issue really is pivotal electoral votes. The current regional cleavages of presidential politics—the marginal status of both the Great Lakes and the Southeast—all but force political attention to the industries there. And strategy to remobilize U.S. industry and regain U.S. global competitiveness will founder unless it reflects sufficient attention to the political geography of blue-collar-worker concentrations and the well-established interest groups of the old industrial belts. The realpolitik is almost just that simple.

Bluntly put, any salable and workable trade and industrial strategy must harness, not condemn, the interests and ambitions of the existing economic lobbies. Like most advanced societies, the United States has a plethora of institutionalized and vested interests. And if Washington is the national capital, it is even more the national interest-group capital. National economic programs that do major violence to existing industrial relationships and lobbying groups usually don't get anywhere. More specifically, no one should doubt that there exists in the interest-group system a lingering bias toward the older basic industries, because it is indeed very substantial. Autos, steel, textiles, paper, chemicals, mining, utilities and the like all have entrenched lobbies and well-developed lines of political influence and communication. High-tech lobbies, by contrast, are just getting started. Ken Hagerty, government relations vice-president of the American Electronics Association, puts it this way: "The electronics industry is not playing a role in the legislative and political activities in this country in proportion to their role in the economy. . . . The flip side is that the smokestack industries have political influence disproportionate to their economic importance to the country."[2]

Moreover, should the survival of basic industry be in jeopardy, even businessmen overcome their distaste for federal-aid programs —such is the ongoing national sense of the importance of basic industry. Polling by the Opinion Research Corporation in the spring of 1983 found sizable majorities of opinion leaders—55 percent among business executives, 75 percent among government officials, 86 percent among labor union leaders—favoring some kind of government involvement to "ensure the survival" of basic industries. Only academicians, by 51 percent to 41 percent, preferred to accept reliance on imports rather than increased government help for our own basic industries.

Organized labor's strong commitment to smokestack enterprise can hardly be overstated. Old-line unions with memberships from basic industries—high tech is barely unionized—have much more clout in present-day Washington, reflecting yesteryear's political glories, than they can expect to deploy in the coming information age. For many AFL-CIO unions, preserving basic industry is a necessity of institutional self-preservation. Futurists may dismiss the AFL-CIO's relationship with the Democratic party as "dinosaurs mating," but pragmatists must accept substantial labor influence as a given for economic policy making in the rest of the 1980s. American unions are afraid—of lost jobs, of lost influence and of a lost way of life.

Given a choice from a policy standpoint, the United Auto Workers, the Steelworkers and the Textile Workers would prefer trade protectionism and federal aid to preserve and subsidize basic industries over anything else. Conversely, their influence would be thrown onto the congressional scales against any Ataripol or free-market blueprint that sought to sacrifice basic industries to advance high tech. That's a political fact of life. Fortunately, the middle ground is that most industrial unions, knowing their strength is fading, appear willing to embrace a compromise view—to ally themselves with industry strategists to advance the consensus goals spelled out by the Labor-Industry Coalition for International Trade, among others. It's worth listing the unions in LICIT: Amalgamated Clothing and Textile Workers Union; Communications Workers of America; International Brotherhood of Electrical Workers; American Flint Glass Workers Union of North America; Industrial Union Department of the AFL-CIO; International Ladies Garment Workers Union; International Association of Machinists and Aerospace Workers; United Paperworkers International Union; United Rubber, Cork, Linoleum and Plastic Workers of America; and United Steelworkers of America. That's the stuff of a sizable coalition.

Of the fifteen points laid out in chapter 4, only a few are out of kilter with real-world, as opposed to rhetorical, union positions. Indeed, the LICIT unions have specifically put forward half the proposals. Economic nationalism is popular with much of labor. Moreover, to the extent—inevitable, I think—that a business agenda must involve changes in labor-management relations, union strategists have an additional reason to be supportive. A collaborative arrangement with industry is in their interest. To be sure, ideological purists—high-tech futurists or ultra-free-market enthusiasts—will become indignant over a policy around which major elements of business and labor can rally. But to enact actual legislation in Washington, the substantial agreement of entrenched business and labor organizations is a plus, not a minus.

In sum, the basis for business and labor agreement on the outlines of a reasonable policy package appears substantial.

INTEREST GROUPS AND THE FUTURE

Establishing a new national trade and industrial strategy with the support of a considerable array of interest groups is one thing; making sure that it will become a vehicle for national economic change in the future is something else. Here I have to admit to an important leap of faith. During the last twenty years, much proposed legislation in Washington has bogged down, sometimes from the start, in interest-group tailoring and exploitation. Professor Mancur Olson, in his fascinating book *The Rise and Decline of Nations*, details all too well how economic civilizations have fallen as a result of accumulating top-heavy interest groups that veto change.[3] It is possible, therefore, that interest groups can co-opt any national trade and industrial strategy in a way that would turn the program into a gravy train with no value to the larger American public. This could happen.

Nevertheless, we have to gamble that we can escape Olson's law, at least in part. We have so many interest groups in this country, and they have a fluidity and flexibility not found elsewhere. Rigidity and atrophy are not inevitable, as they were in Mandarin China or the Ottoman Empire. Indeed, my speculation is that an industrial strategy could be tailored now to appeal to an existing set of dominant interests with the reasonable expectation that the economic institutions, mechanisms and biases created could be partially reoriented during the late 1980s and the 1990s by a changing American industrial lobby.

Fluidity is the key. As high-tech lobbies gain Washington expertise and influence, within a few years they could begin to balance the voices of the basic industries that would dominate a federal Department of International Trade and Industry today. Ditto for the service industries. If anything, establishing the institutions and the new interest-group context of a competitiveness strategy would force high-tech and service industries to intensify their efforts in Washington, efforts that are currently inadequate. Their political presence might then begin to parallel their importance to the future of the nation's economy. In the short run, of course, high-tech industries —from semiconductors and microcomputers to fiber optics—share the stake that basic industries and their lobbies have in mobilizing our vigilance against Japan. And they also have a greater stake in an accelerated commitment to scientific education and scientific research and development, which must be a part of any national economic mobilization.

Strategically, my fifteen-part program is designed to eschew a commitment to any particular technology, region or production mode. To be sure, no major program like this one can be truly neutral. There is time enough, though, to make those commitments after several years' experience with a Department of International Trade and Industry, with more assertive trade-law enforcement, with more sophisticated antitrust thinking, with a better-coordinated economic policy, and with major new outlays for research and education. Critical issues can be confronted then that must now, for political and ideological reasons, be sidestepped. Among them are whether we need some national agency to provide authority and financing for the reconstitution of redundant industries and whether we need a federal-level institution to make decisions on future technologies and to fund their development. In all likelihood, these questions cannot be resolved as we try to implement a first stage in the policy. They may, however, belong to a second stage. If the American public, politicians and even business executives react favorably to a mild incremental level of government involvement in the economy, then perhaps by 1986 or 1987 we may see the creation of a National Steel Authority to help restructure that industry, or a U.S. Advanced Technologies Corporation to target and provide capital to high-technology, high-value-added industries. For the near term, though, dominant American interest groups and opinion molders appear not to want to go that far.

INFUSING HIGH TECH INTO BASIC INDUSTRIES

If political pragmatism dictates substantial early support to the rehabilitation of troubled basic industries like steel, textiles and autos, so do two other considerations. The first—one that we take for granted and that brooks no denial—is national defense. We cannot, for example, afford to import tanks from Korea. Whether we're talking about steel or machine tools, a considerable group of industries have a defense role. A second, related consideration is the extent to which the future of basic industries can be improved by the infusion of high technology. In practical terms, the future of basic industries and that of high-tech industries are really interdependent.

Happily, we have already seen a major shift away from the simplistic notion of high-tech and basic industries as alternative, competing modes of production and poles of political economics. Here, too, policy movement is toward synthesis. In their book *Industrial Renaissance: Producing a Competitive Future for America*, William Abernathy, Kim B. Clark and Alan Kantrow, of the Harvard Business School, argued against what they call the soufflé theory—that an industry, like a soufflé, once risen cannot rise again. Their contrary analysis is that old industries can indeed be reconstructed, up to a point, and that "the only workable solution is for U.S. managers to undertake—and for government to support—efforts to restructure older industries by grounding them on more technologically advanced products and processes."[4] They call this technological rejuvenation a process of "de-maturing." Most of their thinking is about the automobile industry, but there are signs that the same thing can happen in steel. In an interview, Abernathy said, "As far as the future is concerned, my view is we have to have a competitive steel industry. Targeting on high tech as a salvation is a lot of baloney. We have to make basic industries work. We have got to make steel work."[5] Not surprisingly, industry executives agree. In a speech to the Steel Service Center Institute, E. Bradley Jones, chairman of Republic Steel Corporation, went so far as to cite the technological revolution as an opportunity, not a threat: "We are turning increasingly to high technology to improve quality and productivity. Lasers, fiber optics, computer process controls and ladle metallurgy are all showing up to an expanding degree in our plants and mills. . . . No industry has a greater potential for benefitting from progress in high technology than steel."[6]

While that may be too optimistic, the basic thesis is valid—and increasingly recognized. In much the same vein as Abernathy, Clark and Kantrow, Harvard's Robert Reich has also come to reject the idea of an either-or between high tech and basic industries, saying that the real issue is not "smokestack versus high tech. It's how to quickly imbed the high tech in the smokestack."[7]

Similarly, Howard P. Foley, president of the Massachusetts High Technology Council, dismisses the desire for "black and white answers to complicated questions [that] has placed us between an open hearth furnace and a semiconductor."

> It seems some people forget that many high-tech products are being applied in traditional industry settings to improve productivity, lower costs and make products—and the companies that manufacture them—more competitive.
>
> Many high technology companies have already spun intricate webs with many basic industries. Indeed, without the smokestack industry, high tech in this country would find its feet firmly planted in thin air. *Fortune* magazine noted recently that all U.S. businesses devoted half their capital investment to computers, instruments, and electronic and communications systems last year—an increase in high-tech investments from just 25 percent in 1972 and 30 percent in 1977—and many of these investments are being made by basic manufacturing industries such as steel, auto, and rubber. . . .
>
> Basic U.S. industries need to recognize the benefits that are inherent

in many high technology products, and we should be working together to develop policies that encourage the integration of high technology into basic industry. In the long run, this will make both of these industries more competitive and more profitable, and create more good jobs.[8]

Foley's analysis suggests a rather convincing economic, as opposed to merely political, reason for shaping a first-stage industrial strategy to put a major emphasis on basic industries. Basic industries have to be kept vital enough to need (and nurture) advanced technology. Neglect of U.S. basic industries could actually wind up undercutting U.S. high-tech development.

ASSERTIVENESS, NOT BLATANT PROTECTIONISM

Washington policy makers, of course, will have to exercise restraint. Even though our economic strategy must develop a new nationalism and trade law aggressiveness, there are good reasons not to let matters go too far too fast. Up to a point, we will either be putting our own internal economic house in order—with new tax approaches, lower interest rates and changes in labor-management relations—or merely following well-traveled European and Japanese programmatic pathways—by establishing a new Department of International Trade and Industry, relaxing antitrust laws and improving export finance. Either way, our trading partners have little cause to complain. East Asia and Western Europe cannot cry foul when they see imitation. Moreover, there's little doubt about the need to insist upon the setting up of some kind of international forum to adjudicate what kinds of business-government collaboration are acceptable in a new world trading system.

By contrast, we could provoke serious foreign countermeasures by any resort to domestic-content legislation, import quotas and tariff increases—in short, to any of the more extreme measures of protectionism. Realpolitik dictates caution here, not because of any commitment to obsolete models of a global free-trade system but because of our own export vulnerability. Whatever may be true of steel, machine tools or even semiconductors, there are other industries or economic sectors in which the United States routinely runs huge trade surpluses—in agriculture, for example, and in services like banking, transportation, insurance and finance. Companies and individuals in these sectors are working for an increasingly assertive

U.S. policy to overcome foreign barriers and practices and open up new overseas markets, so they are vulnerable to recrimination by foreigners angered by U.S. protection of its basic industries. Countries whose steel, textiles, automobiles or electronics exports are blocked from our markets could easily move to block or reduce American agricultural and service exports. Japan, for example, takes so much of our soybean crop that the soybean is a potential Japanese hostage for our behavior on steel or semiconductors.

Up to the levels of assertiveness recommended in my fifteen points, public opinion polls and a growing array of expert analyses suggest that Washington has no choice but to take a firmer stance on behalf of U.S. interests and industries. More provocative approaches, however, especially where there's a sharp divergence between public enthusiasm and expert reluctance, raise a row of important red flags: recrimination, retaliation and reciprocity. The cost to the United States of going too far could be considerable. New York bankers, Kansas farmers and San Francisco exporters could lose far more than Midwestern steelworkers would gain.

Major elements of organized labor might favor that kind of risk-taking simply because of the enormous stake they have in sustaining the declining basic industries from which they draw their membership. But from a larger national perspective, there's no justification to include such measures as domestic-content legislation or major tariff increases in any competitiveness agenda. Not only would these be provocative and counterproductive in the international trading system, but they would stifle what should also come out of the competitiveness issue—a great national debate and mobilization of public opinion.

Just as voters and opinion makers cannot be expected to get behind implausible futuristic plans for the American political economy, it's hard to see any broad-based consensus forming around the moods and approaches of a commercial yesterday. But a competitiveness strategy—meshing an assertive rather than a narrowly protective economic nationalism with the programmatic agendas of the leading business and research groups—could command enough interest-group backing to move on to what is the real challenge: launching the national debate and national renewal.

CHAPTER
8

A Great Mid-1980s Debate?

We need to talk seriously about competitiveness, not just to restore American economic strength and regain foreign markets, but also to speed an ideological and institutional transition. Without debate and transition, our political culture of two centuries makes it all but impossible for Washington to orchestrate a major readjustment to the world economy. Even with a national consensus, the federal government will face an enormous challenge defining an economic role and involvement to match or even outachieve the activity of competing foreign powers. Shaping a better macroeconomic policy in combination with redefining federal responsibility for promoting our trade and industry may be the ultimate battleground of coming political and legislative expertise.

The sooner serious dialogue and disputation begin, the better. On the one hand, U.S. economic erosion in world markets is hardly good news. The era now ending—the period of mass industrial production and minimal government involvement—was America's heyday. On the other hand, the world-wide upheaval now redistributing industry and technology demands an early and constructive response from our country. Nostalgia cannot bring back the Eisenhower presidency, nor can it keep the question of national competitiveness off the political agenda. Conservatives only kid themselves if they think so. In like manner, liberals only kid themselves if they think that the new political economics signals a return to their traditional mode of operation. One goal of the debate must be to educate the public to reshape its political and economic view of government. In ideological and interest-group terms, the new neointerventionism is just as likely to draw upon Alexander Hamilton and Daniel Webster as on Franklin D. Roosevelt and the New Deal.

Two other reasons for joining a major national debate also go beyond economic programs, statistics and technologies. In the first place, Americans are great achievers when aroused; moreover, it is not only good policy but good politics for the side that links itself to economic renewal in the eyes of the electorate. Second, any new crusade probably must involve setbacks and discomfort for those of our allies—Japan, in particular—whose military and commercial arrangements over the past decade have thrived on a complacency on the part of the United States. We must also confront that question —namely, what should the United States now expect from its allies and alliances?

Additionally, for those conservatives who reject any new federal role, this word of caution: you have a point when you say that if basic economic policy could be set straight—deficits, taxes, interest rates, monetary approaches, exchange rates and all the rest—U.S. industries could come back on their own and would need no government shepherding. In theory, that's true, but in theory only. Politically, however, there's good reason to believe that the same upheaval roiling international trade waters with waves of protectionism and neo-mercantilism is sending similar, if not the same, disruptive currents through fiscal and monetary policy. During the last decade, currency arrangements have come unraveled alongside trade arrangements. And control of the money supply seems elusive everywhere, as does control of government spending in this time of interest-group politics. The bottom line is that, during the last fifteen years, attempts to bring order to macroeconomic policy have proved fruitless. And we have to expect more of the same on that front. The idea of a macroeconomic solution may be illusory.

It may even be fair to characterize proponents of a purely economic-policy–oriented U.S. global approach as macroillusionists. Of course, so are the people who see national industrial policy as a cure-all. Careful, restrained proindustrial strategists, by contrast, should posit business-government collaboration less as an economic remedy than as a necessary counter to the fact that most other countries are already doing it and the rules of international political economics have changed. Nobody's new ideas—nobody's new strategies—are panaceas.

If the attention to an industrial and trade strategy is to yield an effective result, it will come out of compromise, and that is what must be shaped in the debate to come. Sweeping philosophic conviction, most entrenched in the free-market right and in the tired, old-style interventionist mentality of so many liberals, must find some middle ground. There's no room, for instance, for former White House chief policy planner Edwin Harper's response to industrial policy, which was simply to offer Reaganomics, which he claimed was working well. But the Democrats, for their part, have flocked to new theoretical pastures too quickly. In large part, that's because they have had so little success with basic economic policy. Consider this evaluation made in the summer of 1983 by economist Barry Bosworth of the Brookings Institution, himself a Democrat who served as director of the Council on Wage-Price Stability in the Carter administration: "The Democrats don't seem to be interested in that [basic economic policy and growth]. It means dealing with the deficits, taxes and spending. To them, this seems old hat. Their theme seems to be industrial policy and fascination with zero-sum games, economic equity and things like that."[1]

Little national good would come from any debate so defined—stereotyped free-market insistence versus a liberal interventionism that will not address real-world problems. Fortunately, even preliminary maneuvering has brought about modification and amplification of early positions. Serious observers on both sides understand that institutional approaches—changes in antitrust laws, in government structures, in export facilitation, in research and development and education—must be combined with committed attention to fundamental macroeconomic policy problems like deficits, interest rates and exchange rates.

What is cause for worry is how many free-market conservative and interventionist liberal thinkers seem unable to understand the new importance of U.S. economic nationalism. Development of that awareness—and with it, a conspicuous willingness to assert our interests against unacceptable forms of foreign trade barriers and competition—constitutes an essential third leg of any plausible national economic strategy. Simply put, competitiveness has become a political and economic catalyst. To many Americans, unacceptable for-

eign practices are both a problem demanding a response and the basis
of a major move to economic activism. Policy makers should heed
the practical business leaders, who have been a lot quicker than
pundits or economic theoreticians to define what may be the new
center of opinion. Note the following blunt summarization by Raymond Hay, chairman of the LTV Corporation, in a July 1983 newspaper advertisement:

> Those of us who are free marketers suddenly find ourselves calling for
> protectionist trade legislation. Those of us who have endorsed the idea
> that government should "get off our backs" now call for more govern-
> ment involvement. Why this sudden about-face? Clearly, business is
> increasingly aware that in today's global economy the rules have
> changed. That is what the industrial policy dialogue is all about.
>
> For years now, America has virtually alone pursued a free market
> policy, while foreign countries have become increasingly mercantilistic,
> indulging in industrial targeting and unfair competition. In this climate,
> trade has been neither free nor fair, and our basic industries have been
> placed at a severe competitive disadvantage. The American marketplace
> has become a happy hunting ground for government-subsidized foreign
> products, while we have lost our leadership position. The industrial base
> from which we have drawn much of our economic strength is threatened
> as never before.
>
> The imperative is clear: We must change our approach to industrial
> life in this country; we must "reindustrialize" in a global environment.
> If that is a formal or informal industrial policy, so be it.[2]

If rhetoric like this takes over the national debate, the political
forces unleashed could be powerful—the stuff of which mobilizations
are made. By contrast, neither the Republicans' free-market insistence nor the Democrats' New Deal–revisited penchant for reindus-
trialization, investment banks, planning agencies and economic
coordinating councils is likely to stir up much voter enthusiasm.
What counts with the electorate is national competitiveness—making America number one again. It's in harnessing those psychologies,
and not in trying to sell the public some new economic theory, that
an important politics could be generated.

Paradoxically, it's possible that a nationalist arousal of the public
could bring about a broader government involvement in trade and
economic strategy than any half-successful liberal industrial policy
attempt. In part, that's because the electorate could be ripe for a

neomercantilist appeal. By contrast, I'm inclined to think that any liberal political triumph and industrial policy sponsorship in the mid-1980s would be restrained by political and interest-group realities: national business lobbies could probably block any far-reaching proposal, and a moderate-conservative coalition should control the U.S. Senate at least through 1986.

In the face of a possible nationalist surge, debate over a new U.S. economic and trade strategy cannot sidestep the question of our overall relationship with allies like Japan, because a careful evaluation is in order. Much more is at stake than automobiles and transistor radios. On the one hand, Japan is our leading ally in Asia; on the other hand, Japan's present trade impact on our economy is intolerable, not least because Japan escapes a serious defense outlay, enjoying shelter under our military umbrella. Admittedly, part of our approach to Tokyo has to be political and geopolitical. Diplomats say we shouldn't push too hard for agricultural markets that would disrupt Japan's own food producers because Japan's farmers are a prop of the ruling, pro-American political faction. Other U.S. strategists frame a different equation—namely, that we should ease off on Japanese trade concessions if Tokyo will increase its military commitment. But how much longer can the United States continue to subordinate economic self-protection?

Arguably, if U.S. global strategists do not want a breach with Japan, economic tough-mindedness may deserve a higher priority. As economist Lester Thurow has observed: "We just can't afford to siphon off 8 percent to 9 percent of our GNP for the military, while Germany siphons off 3.5 percent and Japan less than 1 percent. If the brightest engineers in Japan are designing video recorders and the brightest engineers in the United States are designing MX missiles, then we shouldn't find it surprising that they conquer the video recorder market."[3]

Not, of course, that the video-recorder market is the major problem. What is really at stake is continued U.S. dominance of domestic and foreign high-technology markets. Unless the government adopts an aggressive trade and economic strategy, these markets could be lost to Japan. This, in turn, could ruin U.S.–Japanese relations. That point was underscored in testimony before Congress in June 1983 by ex-CIA Deputy Director Bobby Inman, now director of the Microelectronics and Computer Technology Corporation, the research consortium mentioned earlier. Inman said that "we have to keep in focus that international trade is an integral part of our national security and helps hold our alliance together," and that unless U.S. firms are able to remain competitive, "we may become involved in trade wars, which could lead to the break-up of our alliance."[4] In his new book, *The Amazing Race*, University of Virginia Professor William H. Davidson argues that the current techno-rivalry with Japan is just as important as the arms race with the Soviets.[5] The point, of course, is that serious, stepped-up economic pressure on Japan may actually be necessary to maintain the basis of our Pacific alliance.

At the same time, there's no doubt that anger at Japan—as well as fear for the U.S. economic future—has the potential to be a major rallying cry for Americans. Our leaders, in the meantime, have a narrow line to walk. Channeled in the right economic and institutional directions, national frustration could even be a catalyst for convincing business, labor, politicians and the public to support institutional innovations that would otherwise have been decades in the making. Something like that happened in Germany a century ago, spurred by national demand to compete with Britain. According to British economic historian Christopher Freeman,

> When Britain had the industrial revolution, the Germans were very, very worried. [Georg Friedrich] List, who was the leading German economist at that time, was most impressed by the contrast with what was the Japan of that day—Britain. He wanted Germany to imitate England.
>
> And, of course, there were a lot of Germans who said, We can't imitate England. We have all these principalities. We have the Free States of Hamburg and Lübeck. We have Bavaria and Prussia, and so on, and it led to the German unification movement, an enormous social change. It also led to a massive effort pushed by List to introduce massive technical education on a scale surpassing Britain. They did it, and had the best system of technical education in the second half of the 19th Century. They did it to overtake Britain.[6]

The United States, of course, is not in the same position with respect to Japan as the Germany of a century ago was with respect to Britain. We may be the fading power. But given the sentiments expressed in the media and in public opinion surveys, the economic threat that Americans perceive in Japan and East Asia could spark a resurgence of U.S. competitiveness. In fact, fierce debate over and reaction to the Japanese challenge are probably a precondition of our economic mobilization.

All in all, it's hard to see how the United States can fail to profit from the new political and economic dialogue. As American Business Conference Chairman Arthur Levitt has observed,

> one little noted but potentially significant advantage of the industrial policy debate is that it has triggered a dialogue involving virtually every interest and outlook in America. If there is to be an industrial policy, everyone will be affected; everyone will have a stake—and hopefully a voice—in its formulation. The process of debating, formulating and implementing policies of growth and opportunity could become the catalyst that enables our workers and businessmen, our industrialists and academics, to form a partnership—not to direct and control our economy, but to hammer out options and strive for consensus on broad objectives worthy of America.[7]

I couldn't agree more.

Notes

Introduction

1. Theodore White, *America in Search of Itself*, quoted in "Limited Protection of Trade Is Vital," Los Angeles *Times*, April 12, 1983.
2. Bernard Mitchell, "Trade with Japan Needs New Rules," *Business Week*, May 23, 1983.
3. William Krist, "The U.S. Response to Foreign Industrial Policies," *National Journal*, January 22, 1983.
4. "High Tech Now Has Its Critics," Philadelphia *Inquirer*, March 28, 1983.
5. *International Trade, Industrial Policies and the Future of American Industry* (Washington, D.C.: Labor-Industry Coalition for International Trade, 1983), p. iv (hereafter cited as LICIT).
6. Bernard J. O'Keefe, "We Did It to Ourselves," Boston *Globe*, July 5, 1983.
7. "Just What Is a NIP?," *Industry Week*, June 27, 1983.

Chapter 1

1. Louis Harris speech to Yale Political Union, reprinted in the Los Angeles *Times*, September 27, 1981.
2. Robert B. Reich, *The Next American Frontier* (New York: Times Books, 1983).
3. "U.S. Gains in Technology," New York *Times*, September 9, 1983.

4. LICIT, pp. 4–7.
5. Ibid., p. 1.
6. Ibid., p. 72.
7. Ibid., p. 24.
8. "Reagan Acts to Protect Specialty Steel," Washington *Times*, July 6, 1983.
9. LICIT, p. 54.
10. "Textile Executive Calls for Lid on Chinese Imports," Chicago *Tribune*, April 8, 1983.
11. Ibid.
12. "Government Must Play Bigger Role in Pushing U.S. Products," Los Angeles *Times*, August 9, 1982.
13. "Japan Tops the Field in High-Speed Computers," Boston *Globe*, February 7, 1984.
14. "International Scene," *Industry Week*, February 20, 1984.
15. Adapted from LICIT, p. 18.
16. "How Japan Helps Its Industry," New York *Times*, May 18, 1983.
17. *The Effect of Japanese Government Targeting on World Semiconductor Competition* (Cupertino, Cal.: Semiconductor Industry Association, 1983).
18. Ronald Shelp, "Servicing the Service Sector," Boston *Globe*, April 12, 1983.
19. "The Next Trade Crisis May Be Just Around the Corner," *Business Week*, March 19, 1984.
20. "Industrial Policy Debate," Boston *Globe*, May 15, 1983.
21. "Why the Democrats Need to Come Up with an Industrial Policy," *Business Week*, November 21, 1983.
22. "Doubts on Industrial Policy," New York *Times*, October 15, 1983.
23. Robert Samuelson, "High Tech Hysteria as Industrial Policy," Washington *Post*, April 26, 1983.
24. "U.S. Must Work to Gain World Trade," Louisville *Courier-Journal*, April 24, 1983.
25. Michael Evans, "Fixed Exchange Rates No Panacea," Los Angeles *Times*, May 31, 1983.
26. "Dollar Fever Infects the World," *Business Week*, June 27, 1983.
27. "High Investment Capital Cost Hurting U.S. Industry," Boston *Globe*, April 27, 1983.

Chapter 2

1. "High Tech Development Called Top U.S. Priority," Dallas *News*, April 15, 1983.

2. "Political Realities Ignored," Philadelphia *Inquirer*, May 4, 1983.
3. "Outlook for World Trade Gloomy," Dallas *News*, April 17, 1983.
4. William Ebenstein, *Great Political Thinkers* (New York: Rinehart and Company, 1956), p. 346.
5. Alvin Toffler, *Previews and Premises* (New York: William Morrow, 1983), p. 51.
6. Ibid., p. 19.
7. John Naisbitt, *Megatrends* (New York: Warner Books, 1983).
8. "Protectionism vs. Free Trade," New York *Times*, April 8, 1983.
9. Robert B. Reich, "Beyond Free Trade," *Foreign Affairs*, Spring 1983, p. 774.
10. Robert Heilbroner, "Does Capitalism Have a Future?," *The New York Times Magazine*, August 15, 1982.
11. "Trade: No Nation Has Clean Hands," Los Angeles *Times*, January 31, 1983, p. 12.
12. Ibid.
13. Ibid.
14. "Free Trade Really Isn't," Los Angeles *Times*, April 15, 1983.
15. Paul Kennedy, "Facing Up to Our Decline," Charlotte *Observer*, November 14, 1982.
16. "A Protectionist Temper to the Times," Boston *Globe*, December 19, 1982.
17. Ibid., p. 15.
18. "U.S. Move Worries Japanese," New York *Times*, December 27, 1982.
19. Indianapolis *Star*, April 17, 1983.
20. "Change in U.S. Values Found as Prestige Drops," Houston *Chronicle*, February 14, 1982.
21. LICIT, p. 4.
22. "A Protectionist Temper," loc. cit.
23. Peter Drucker, "Our Industrial Exports Should Weigh on Policy," *Wall Street Journal*, April 21, 1983.
24. "Du Pont Chief Urges Industrial Strategy," Boston *Globe*, December 14, 1983.
25. Richard P. Simmons, "The Contradictions of Free Trade," September 22, 1983 (speech).

Chapter 3

1. "Du Pont Chief Urges Industrial Strategy," loc. cit.
2. John C. Marous, "America Losing Trading Game," Tulsa *World*, December 18, 1983.

3. "Fall Meeting Focuses on Competitiveness," *Trade and Industry* (NAM), November 18, 1983.
4. "Broad U.S. Strategy for High Tech Is Urged," Baltimore *Sun*, March 14, 1983.
5. "Industry Blames Protectionism on U.S.," Chicago *Tribune*, December 20, 1982.
6. "Faith in Free Trade Has Not Waned," *Business Week*, May 30, 1983.
7. *Business & Public Affairs Fortnightly*, January 15, 1983, p. 6.
8. Ibid.
9. LICIT, pp. 57–66.
10. Coalition for International Trade Equity, release, February 15, 1983.
11. *The Effect of Japanese Government Targeting on World Semiconductor Competition.*
12. "U.S. Industrial Policy Cries Out for Definition," Louisville *Courier-Journal*, July 3, 1983.
13. "What Role Will Government Play in High Tech?," *Iron Age*, August 1, 1983.
14. "Testimony of ECAT Executive Vice Chairman Robert L. McNeill before U.S. House Committee on Energy and Commerce," June 22, 1983.
15. *Productivity Policy: Key to the Nation's Economic Future* (New York: Committee for Economic Development, 1983).
16. "New U.S. Push for Competitiveness in World Marketplace Urged," New York *Times*, May 16, 1983.
17. Ibid.
18. O'Keefe, "We Did It to Ourselves," loc. cit.
19. Arthur Levitt, "Industrial Policy: Slogan or Solution," draft manuscript (September 1983).
20. "Threats to U.S. in Technology," New York *Times*, April 15, 1983.
21. "Unemployment Public Enemy No. 1," *Washington Report*, May 9, 1983.
22. "Americans Want Trade Barriers against Japan," Los Angeles *Times*, May 22, 1983.
23. *The Emerging Consensus: Public Attitudes on America's Ability to Compete in the World* (New York: Union Carbide Corporation, 1981), p. 47.
24. *Vital Consensus* (New York: Union Carbide Corporation, 1980).
25. "Unemployment Public Enemy No. 1," loc. cit.
26. Ibid.

Chapter 4

1. "States Fostering High Technology," New York *Times*, August 17, 1983.
2. Neal Pierce, "Dukakis Leads the Way," Boston *Globe*, September 4, 1983.
3. "At Last, Hope for a Coherent Policy," New York *Times*, June 19, 1983.
4. Simmons, op. cit.
5. "The Turf Fight That Threatens the Trade Policy," *Business Week*, May 16, 1983.
6. *The Emerging Consensus*, p. 35.
7. "Danforth Defends Congressional Trade Shift," Richmond *Times-Dispatch*, April 24, 1983.
8. "Faith in Free Trade Has Not Waned," *Business Week*, May 30, 1983.
9. "Trade Agency Plan Raises Questions on Capitol Hill," Richmond *Times-Dispatch*, May 8, 1983.
10. LICIT, p. 58.
11. Conversation with Ambassador Brock, January 18, 1984.
12. *The Emerging Consensus*, p. 42.
13. LICIT, p. 98.
14. "U.S. Seeks Role in Japanese Planning," Los Angeles *Times*, May 23, 1983.
15. *The Emerging Consensus*, p. 45.
16. LICIT, p. 60.
17. "Europe's Desperate Try for High-Tech Teamwork," *Business Week*, May 30, 1983.
18. LICIT, p. 62.
19. *Perspectives on Productivity: A Global View* (Stevens Point, Wis.: Sentry Insurance, 1981).
20. *The Emerging Consensus*, p. 41.
21. "Business' Coming Victory on Exports," *Fortune*, July 25, 1983.
22. The data appear in *The Emerging Consensus*, pp. 31 and 35; *Business Week*, January 31, 1983, p. 97; and the Los Angeles *Times*, May 22, 1983, p. 23.
23. Washington Report, *Florida Trend*, May 1983.
24. "U.S. Needs to Play Hardball with Japan," Indianapolis *Star*, April 17, 1983.
25. "U.S. Job Opens Door to Big Profit," Chicago *Tribune*, March 8, 1982.

26. "Foreign Lobbyists," *U.S. News & World Report*, March 29, 1982.

27. "Japan Lobby," Detroit *News*, May 2, 1982, p. 1.

28. Ibid., p. 16.

29. "Americans for Sale," Chicago *Tribune*, March 7, 1982, p. 10.

30. "Yanks Help Japan Make Big U.S. Profits," Chicago *Tribune*, March 10, 1982, p. 10.

31. "Japan Lobby," p. 16.

32. "Should Tax System Encourage Savings?," *Christian Science Monitor*, June 22, 1983.

33. "Dow Surge Helps," Richmond *Times-Dispatch*, May 1, 1983.

34. "Missouri Plant Is Revolutionary," Baltimore *Sun*, May 8, 1983.

35. "Labor Is Down," Des Moines *Register*, April 24, 1983.

36. LICIT, p. 66.

37. "Borman: Wages Should Hinge on Industry Profits," Philadelphia *Inquirer*, June 16, 1983.

38. "A Duty to Invest in Human Capital," Hartford *Courant*, April 3, 1983.

39. "Motivation Is Key," Dallas *News*, June 26, 1983.

40. *Business & Public Affairs Fortnightly*, August 1, 1983, p. 2.

41. W. L. Batt, "Canada's Good Example," *Harvard Business Review*, July/August 1983.

42. "Grasping the New Unemployment," *Fortune*, May 16, 1983.

43. "U.S. Policymakers Fail to Meet Workers' Needs," Chicago *Tribune*, December 2, 1982.

44. "Workplace: Site of Latest Revolution," Los Angeles *Times*, April 24, 1983, p. 12.

45. "Grasping the New Unemployment," p. 110.

46. Ibid., p. 111.

47. Ibid., p. 110.

48. "U.S. Policymakers Fail to Meet Workers' Needs," loc. cit.

49. "Grasping the New Unemployment," p. 112.

50. "Industrial Policy Debate," Boston *Globe*, May 15, 1983.

51. "High Tech Leaves Home," Washington *Post*, May 1, 1983.

52. "U.S. Gaining in Efforts to Stem Loss of High Tech," New York *Times*, April 30, 1983.

53. "House Investigators," Boston *Globe*, June 28, 1983.

54. "The Copyright War That's Brewing with Japan," *Business Week*, February 13, 1984.

55. "Japan Patenting New Approach," Dallas *News*, November 28, 1983.

56. Ibid.

57. "Study Asserts Quality of Schools Presents Economic Threat," New York *Times*, May 5, 1983.

58. "Dallas, Inc., Must Get Smart," Dallas *News*, May 14, 1983.
59. "High Tech Had Message for Reagan," Boston *Globe*, January 28, 1983.
60. "High Tech Gets Even Smarter," Boston *Globe*, April 10, 1983.

Chapter 5

1. William Letwin, *The Origins of Scientific Economics* (Garden City, N.Y.: Doubleday/Anchor Books, 1965), p. 194.
2. Richard Morris, *The Basic Ideas of Alexander Hamilton* (New York: Pocket Books, 1957), p. xvi.
3. Ralph Nader, Mark Green and Joel Seligman, *Taming the Giant Corporation* (New York: W. W. Norton, 1976), p. 14.
4. Ibid.
5. Lawrence M. Friedman, *A History of American Law* (New York: Simon & Schuster, 1973), pp. 169–70.
6. George Rogers Taylor, *The Economic History of the United States*, Vol. 4, *1815–60* (New York: Harper Torchbook, 1968), p. 352.
7. Ibid.
8. LICIT, p. 27.
9. LICIT, p. 28.
10. "Britain Launches Plan," *Christian Science Monitor*, July 8, 1983.
11. Morris, p. 283.
12. "Role of Telecommunications in Industrial Planning Grows," New York *Times,* May 2, 1983.

Chapter 6

1. "Atarizing Reagan," New York *Times*, March 1, 1983.
2. "Seeds of Party Discontent: Political Power Moves West," Tulsa *World*, April 11, 1982.
3. "The Neo-Liberals Push Their Own Brand of Reform," *Business Week*, January 21, 1983.
4. Kevin P. Phillips, *Mediacracy* (New York: Doubleday, 1975), p. 41.
5. Naisbitt, p. 72.
6. Robert Kuttner, "Economic Jeopardy," *Mother Jones*, May 1982, p. 30.
7. "The Neo-Liberals Push Their Own Brand of Reform," p. 98.
8. New York *Times*, October 3, 1982.
9. "High Tech Now Has Its Critics," Philadelphia *Inquirer*, March 28, 1983.
10. "Midwest Message," Milwaukee *Journal*, May 29, 1983.
11. "Millions of Jobs," Atlanta *Journal*, July 3, 1983.

12. Gerald W. McEntee, "Is High Tech Unpatriotic?," Washington *Post*, July 10, 1983.

13. "High Tech Charging Onto World Scene," Boston *Globe*, June 27, 1983.

14. "Mass. High Technology: Glamor, Growth, Few Blacks," Boston *Globe*, April 25, 1983.

15. Bruce Bartlett, "The Old Politics of a New Industrial Policy," *Wall Street Journal*, April 19, 1983.

16. "Americans for Trade Barriers against Japan," Los Angeles *Times*, May 22, 1983.

17. "Views of Japan Worsen," New York *Times*, April 6, 1982.

18. Krist, op. cit.

19. Penn-Schoen (Garth Analysis), 1983.

20. "The Neo-Liberals Push Their Own Brand of Reform," loc. cit.

21. Richard Fisher, "Growing Thrust of Sun Belt Shifting Foreign Policy," Dallas *News*, June 17, 1983.

Chapter 7

1. William Safire, *The New Language of Politics* (New York: Macmillan, Collier Books, 1972), p. 25.

2. *Business & Public Affairs Fortnightly*, February 1, 1983, p. 5.

3. Mancur Olson, *The Rise and Decline of Nations* (New Haven: Yale University Press, 1982).

4. William Abernathy, Kim B. Clark and Alan Kantrow, *Industrial Renaissance: Producing a Competitive Future for America* (New York: Basic Books, 1983).

5. "A Rusty Industry," Philadelphia *Inquirer*, August 2, 1983.

6. "Steel's High Tech Opportunity," *Industry Week*, May 30, 1983.

7. "Selling America on the Reich Stuff," Washington *Post*, July 6, 1983.

8. Howard P. Foley, "The Future as Seen from Route 128," Boston *Globe*, March 29, 1983.

Chapter 8

1. "Democrats' Industrial Policy Charades as Economic Program," Chicago *Tribune*, July 31, 1983.

2. Advertisement by LTV Corporation, entitled "America's Basic Industries: Is an Industrial Policy Their Salvation?" in the *Wall Street Journal*, July 28, 1983.

3. "Industrial Policy Debate," Boston *Globe*, May 15, 1983.

4. Dallas *News*, September 15, 1983.
5. William H. Davidson, *The Amazing Race* (New York: John Wiley & Sons, 1983).
6. "An Interview with Christopher Freeman," *Forbes*, June 20, 1983.
7. Arthur Levitt, op. cit.

About the Author

KEVIN P. PHILLIPS, author, lawyer, commentator and publisher, was born in New York City in 1940 and educated at Colgate University, the University of Edinburgh and Harvard Law School. In 1968, he served as chief political/voting patterns analyst in the Republican presidential campaign and thereafter published *The Emerging Republican Majority.* He is currently president of the American Political Research Corporation, publisher of the *American Political Report* and the *Business & Public Affairs Fortnightly*, a consultant to several leading investment firms and a frequent press and broadcast commentator. He and his wife and two children live in Bethesda, Maryland, and West Goshen, Connecticut.